This journal belongs to

....

CAREY SCOTT

Your Best Day

DEVOTIONAL JOURNAL

180
**Encouraging
Readings
from
God's Word**

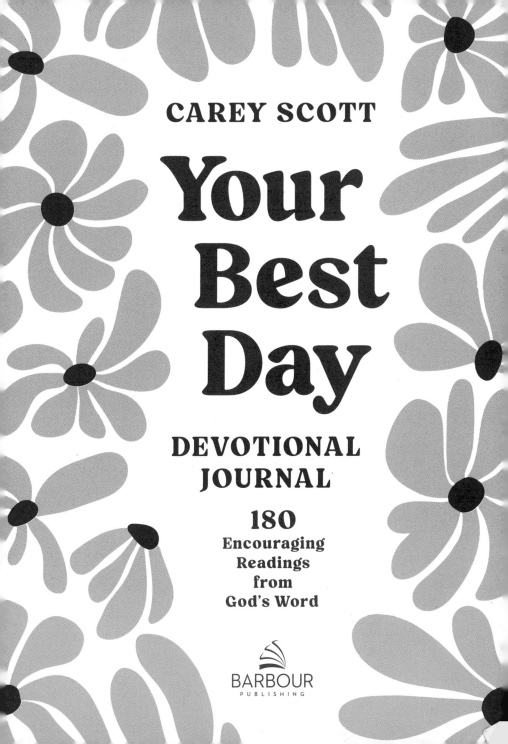

BARBOUR
PUBLISHING

Published by Barbour Publishing, Inc., 1810 Barbour Drive, Uhrichsville, Ohio 44683, www.barbourbooks.com

Our mission is to inspire the world with the life-changing message of the Bible.

Member of the
Evangelical Christian
Publishers Association

Printed in China.

Introduction

Every good day begins with a prayer. Talking to God as you go about your busyness helps make your day even better. And, as you drift off to sleep sharing your heart with the Father, it makes for the *very best* day. So let the Lord be your constant companion.

No matter the challenges or celebrations, He wants to be part of the conversation. God wants to hear it all—straight from your mouth. Whether annoyed or awestruck, jolted or joyous, hurt or happy. . . share it with Him. Let your feelings flow as you unpack the day in your own words. Then watch as the worries melt away. Experience God's delight as you talk about your excitement. Embrace the direction downloaded as you receive His guidance. My friend, that's how you set yourself up to have the best day...*ever*.

Always Begin with God

Now may God, the fountain of hope, fill you to overflowing with
uncontainable joy and perfect peace as you trust in him.
And may the power of the Holy Spirit continually surround your
life with his super-abundance until you radiate with hope!
ROMANS 15:13 TPT

Your best days always begin with God. Even in the hardest seasons, it's possible to live with a sense of joy and peace. When you're overwhelmed, hurting, angry, or grieving, placing your hope in God changes things. Your decision to go to Him first enables you to experience an abundance of goodness directly because of God's presence.

As believers, it's important we embrace all this life of faith affords us. We're not weak or wimpy. God adds His *super* to our *natural*, and the results are extraordinary. The Lord's Spirit fuels our hope as we trust Him with our worries and concerns. And that's what helps us live our very best life, no matter what.

....

....

....

....

....

....

....

....

God, help me remember You're the key to my joy and peace.
You're the reason I can have hope even when times are tough.
Let me start each day in Your presence. In Jesus' name. Amen.

Just Around the Corner

Do not forget to rejoice, for hope is always just around the corner. Hold up through the hard times that are coming, and devote yourselves to prayer.
ROMANS 12:12 VOICE

Sometimes we need a reminder that hope is right around the corner. We need to remember it's available to us through faith, not hidden from believers. There are moments when life feels so overwhelming that our desperation is poured out through tears and prayers. Let God be the one to build the expectation that you're seen—and in His presence—right now.

There's comfort in knowing these things. Friend, you're not alone because He's with you always. Even when surrounded by a loving community of supporters, they're no substitute for God's goodness. He's the hope you can count on without fail. He is the strength that holds you up through hard times. God is the maker of good days. Trust Him.

....

....

....

....

....

....

....

*God, I don't always understand the details of Your plan or methodology of Your timing, but I know You're good, no matter what.
Help me rejoice in the waiting, believing Your revelation is right around the corner. In Jesus' name. Amen.*

Having a Faith-Filled Focus

Be cheerful with joyous celebration in every season of life. Let your joy overflow!
PHILIPPIANS 4:4 TPT

Of course, you can bank on good days and joyous seasons and cheerful moments when things are going your way. When your needs are being met and your plans are panning out without a hitch, it's not difficult to navigate your schedule with a smile. Being pleasant and hopeful is easy when pleasantries are happening and hope is abounding. Wouldn't you agree?

But today's verse often feels like a tall order. And the truth is even the most seasoned believer can struggle to find joy in times of trouble and pain. It's during those moments that we want to hide under the covers. However, the Bible has countless verses that encourage us to have a faith-filled focus through life's hardships. With faith, we can rise above our circumstances and have an awesome day because we know God is already there, making a way for our joy to overflow regardless.

God, I'm going to need Your help walking out this verse.
Give me confidence to be hopeful in every season,
no matter what. In Jesus' name. Amen.

The Power of Perspective

Consider it a sheer gift, friends, when tests and challenges come at you from all sides. You know that under pressure, your faith-life is forced into the open and shows its true colors. So don't try to get out of anything prematurely. Let it do its work so you become mature and well-developed, not deficient in any way.
JAMES 1:2–4 MSG

Want to live with a hopeful heart? Then let God's Word mold your perspective. Because when you let scripture shape your mindset, you'll begin to see life through the lens of faith. And although it may be countercultural to what the world says to think and feel, God's Word applied will settle your spirit as it grows your trust in Him.

You'll begin to see the silver lining in hardships. Your heart will rest, knowing God is at work through the disappointments. And you'll be at peace in the middle of chaos. Let the Lord be your comfort so you can live each day in victory!

....

....

....

....

....

....

....

....

God, help me see each challenge and test from a godly perspective.
Hold me tighter than any pressure the world brings.
Grow me through adversity! In Jesus' name. Amen.

Maturing the Fruits

But the fruit produced by the Holy Spirit within you is divine love in all its varied expressions: joy that overflows, peace that subdues, patience that endures, kindness in action, a life full of virtue, faith that prevails, gentleness of heart, and strength of spirit. Never set the law above these qualities, for they are meant to be limitless.

GALATIANS 5:22–23 TPT

Once we accept Jesus, the Spirit begins to cultivate these "fruits" in us. They aren't ripe and ready in that regenerated moment; rather, their maturing becomes a beautiful process that can take years to complete.

The truth is that the process of the Spirit growing them to ripeness is often challenging. We are molded through adversity. We are transformed through struggles. But when we recognize each hardship as being divinely used to make us more like Christ, we find comfort. And that's what enables us to have good days, regardless of the growing pains.

....

....

....

....

....

....

....

....

....

God, thank You for loving me so much that Your plan is to mature me into the woman You intend me to be. Help me see each challenge through the lens of faith. In Jesus' name. Amen.

Ask Away

"Until now you've not been bold enough to ask the Father for a single thing
in my name, but now you can ask, and keep on asking him! And you can be
sure that you'll receive what you ask for, and your joy will have no limits!"
JOHN 16:24 TPT

The Word encourages every believer to ask God for the things we need. Yes, He already knows what's on our hearts; but like any loving parent, God wants to hear it from our mouths. He wants a relationship with His beloved! So we're told to ask for what we want. And it's not a once-and-done request. Instead, today's verse is specific when it says to "keep on asking."

Let's remember God is God and not a genie in a bottle. Our wish is not His command. And while He clearly wants us to share requests authentically, we must then trust how and when the Lord answers. We may not get the exact things we ask for, but we'll get exactly what He knows is best for us. Our joy can persist every day as we wait for God's perfect answers!

....

....

....

....

....

....

....

....

....

....

God, I trust Your answers! In Jesus' name. Amen.

Choosing Cheer

A cheerful disposition is good for your health;
gloom and doom leave you bone-tired.
PROVERBS 17:22 MSG

If your aim is to have the very best day, then choose to be cheery rather than gloomy. It doesn't make all your problems go away. It won't fix what's broken nor will it take away any validity of your pain and suffering. But scripture says your health will be blessed by your efforts.

Before your feet hit the floor, ask God to help your outlook on the day be hopeful. Ask for peace in your spirit so your countenance can be calm even though your life feels chaotic. Let Him replenish your strength, and resolve to leave a loving footprint in the lives of others. With God's help, you'll be able to rise above the stress and strife. You will find a confidence unmatched by anything the world offers. And no worry will be able to override your faith-filled response to everything the day brings.

....
....
....
....
....
....
....
....

God, give me the courage to choose cheer over gloom even
when I don't feel it. Let my life model faith so others
will come to know You. In Jesus' name. Amen.

Following His Lead

Now you've got my feet on the life path, all radiant from the shining
of your face. Ever since you took my hand, I'm on the right way.
PSALM 16:11 MSG

There is no life like a life surrendered to the Lord. In every way, the best day on your own is unmatched by a day in God's will. And the counterfeit offerings from the world will only lead you in the opposite direction. What the world offers may be flashy and fun and flattering; but in the end, you'll be left empty-handed and disappointed.

Be it family, friends, finances, fitness, and everything in between, let the Father place your feet on His path for your life. Whether concerned or celebratory, stay in God's presence without straying to the left or right. Your best days will come to be when you're holding His hand and following His lead.

....

....

....

....

....

....

....

....

....

God, forgive me for looking for happiness and joy in all the wrong places.
I confess that my heart has been unconvinced of Your trustworthiness.
From today forward, my only desire is to walk the path that
leads to Your plan for my life. In Jesus' name. Amen.

Replaced with Joy

"In the same way that a woman labors in great pain during childbirth only to forget the intensity of the pain when she holds her child, when I return, your labored grief will also change into a joy that cannot be stolen."
JOHN 16:21–22 VOICE

What a relief to know that when we see Jesus face-to-face, we won't even remember the pain we've had to endure! The moment we take our last breath here on earth, we leave with it every heartbreak. That truth deserves a big fist pump, friend. Because chances are we've walked some very difficult paths in this life. We've suffered greatly. But all of it goes away to be replaced with unconditional joy.

Live today with that powerful perspective. Regardless of what you're facing, praise God it will be redeemed. Let today be glorious, knowing any discomfort is temporary. There is an end date to all misery. And the worries of life here on earth will melt away the moment we see the Lord.

....

....

....

....

....

....

....

....

God, I'm grateful for the opportunity to leave any painful memories behind once I see You! All offenses gone. Grief removed. And I'll exchange it all for joy! In Jesus' name. Amen.

Single-Mindedly

God's kingdom isn't a matter of what you put in your stomach, for goodness' sake. It's what God does with your life as he sets it right, puts it together, and completes it with joy. Your task is to single-mindedly serve Christ. Do that and you'll kill two birds with one stone: pleasing the God above you and proving your worth to the people around you.
ROMANS 14:17–18 MSG

How can you single-mindedly serve God today? It undoubtedly requires steadfast focus, keeping your eyes on the Lord over everything else. At work, glorify Him with your integrity. As you manage kids through school, practice, and homework, be His hands and feet. When you get bad news or have difficult conversations, pray for His help as you navigate each with love and compassion. And when He prompts you to intervene in circumstances, do so with grace and humility.

Being intentional in these ways allows you to please God and reveal your worth to others. It's not for prideful purposes but rather to affirm your faithfulness to His will and ways.

....

....

....

....

....

....

....

....

God, help my heart always be focused on serving You through my words and actions. In Jesus' name. Amen.

The Command to Love

My commandment to you is this: love others as I have loved you.
There is no greater way to love than to give your life for your friends.
JOHN 15:12–13 VOICE

Every day, let's strive to be women who are intentional with our love. It's not only a command, it's a powerful way to let others know they matter. And living with compassion toward others keeps the focus off ourselves. It keeps us facing outward rather than being hyper-sensitive to meeting our own needs.

In what ways do you show your love? Are you quick to listen when someone needs to share their heart? Are you a gift-giver, often charitable with thoughtful trinkets? Do you invest your time in the lives of others? Are you generous with financial resources? Each day, train your eyes to see ways to be full of compassion and care. Be a woman who loves well.

....

....

....

....

....

....

....

....

....

God, help me slow down so I'm able to see those who need
love. Make me aware. Open my heart to be generous and
kind in the right way—and at the right time—to those
You call me to love. In Jesus' name. Amen.

Joy in the Morning

His wrath, you see, is fleeting, but His grace lasts a lifetime. The deepest pains may linger through the night, but joy greets the soul with the smile of morning.

PSALM 30:5 VOICE

Scripture tells us that every morning, we are refueled with joy. Somehow, supernaturally, God restores a weary soul, giving us the beautiful opportunity to have a wonderful day. This isn't fake joy to bury the real troubles we face. We aren't just being brave and hoping things change. The truth is you truly can experience joy in the middle of your mess.

When you activate your faith and place your trust in the Lord, you'll have a unique perspective on your circumstances. You'll experience peace that makes no sense to the world. You'll be comforted *through* the chaos and calamity. And each morning—because of your loving Father—you'll have another opportunity to release the pain and embrace joy, carrying it throughout the day.

....

....

....

....

....

....

....

....

....

God, I want this promise for myself. Too often I wake up weary. Help me grab hold of this promise each morning and choose joy over stress and fear. In Jesus' name. Amen.

He's the Capstone

Thank you for responding to me; you've truly become my salvation!
The stone the masons discarded as flawed is now the capstone!
This is GOD's work. We rub our eyes—we can hardly believe it!
PSALM 118:21–23 MSG

In architecture, the capstone is placed on the top of a structure. It's the final stone in the project and is designed to hold everything together. Jesus is the capstone mentioned in today's verses. And, just as a capstone does in an architectural build, our capstone holds our life together and secures our salvation.

Carry this important truth with you every day. When you're overwhelmed, remember the Lord will hold you together so you can rise to the occasion. He's the one who will give you strength and wisdom. Jesus' role in your life is to be your Savior—not only from your sins but also from your circumstances. You don't have to live in defeat, friend. Let the gift of salvation be what encourages your resolve here and now.

....

....

....

....

....

....

....

....

God, thank You for being my capstone! You're the one
who has the power to hold me together when I feel
weak and weary. In Jesus' name. Amen.

Since God Made Today

This is the day the Eternal God has made; let us celebrate and be happy today.
PSALM 118:24 VOICE

Because God has made today, we can be happy. The fact that He has seen fit to make these next twenty-four hours possible is reason for celebration. If scripture supports this truth, then it's something we must embrace.

You may be having a difficult week. There may be legit reasons for your grief. Maybe you're facing a joy-draining situation that has you in the pit of despair. As imperfect humans living in an imperfect and fallen world, we most definitely have uphill battles to face every single day. But, according to the scripture above, we can still celebrate and be happy because this is the day God has made. And honestly, He is the only one who can create a grateful heart in us even when we're struggling. So ask Him for it. Choose to see God's goodness in what today brings.

....

....

....

....

....

....

....

....

....

God, I want to be a blessing to others. Fill me with joy and excitement so I'm able to embrace today with the right heart. Thank You for all You've planned for me! In Jesus' name. Amen.

Seeing God's Hand

You love him passionately although you have not seen him,
but through believing in him you are saturated with an ecstatic
joy, indescribably sublime and immersed in glory.

1 PETER 1:8 TPT

We live in a world where seeing is believing. From a young age, we've been conditioned to not trust what we can't see with our own eyes. But that's not true with our faith. Faith is believing in something we cannot see. The truth is, however, as believers, we *can* see God's fingerprints all over our life. And that has a powerful way of deepening our love for our heavenly Father.

Think about it. Where have you seen God move in your life? Who has He healed? Where has He provided? How has God saved you or someone you love? What has been restored? What doors have been miraculously opened or closed? When you start to look for God's hand moving in your circumstances, you'll experience an ecstatic joy nothing else can match.

....

....

....

....

....

....

....

....

God, I'm going to start looking for You in my circumstances.
Give me the eyes to see Your love displayed in
my life every day. In Jesus' name. Amen.

This Day Is Special

Go back to your homes, and prepare a feast. Bring out the best food and drink you have, and welcome all to your table, especially those who have nothing. This day is special. It is sacred to our Lord. Do not grieve over your past mistakes. Let the Eternal's own joy be your protection!
NEHEMIAH 8:10 VOICE

Ezra was instructing the Israelites to recognize the day as being special. His command came during the time when Jerusalem's wall, temple, and community were being restored. Ezra was asking his countrymen to commemorate the moment.

In the same way, we can also set apart certain days that matter to us, finding ways to celebrate and memorialize them. It may help us process the pain or celebrate a victory. It may be a reminder of an important moment in your family history or serve as a way of honoring a big decision. Regardless, choose to be intentional to recognize special days and the meaning behind them. God made them notable and special for a reason.

....

....

....

....

....

....

....

....

God, help me know the days to make special, and let me honor the part You played to make them so. In Jesus' name. Amen.

God Fills You

You have filled me with joy, and happiness has risen in my heart, great delight and unrivaled joy, even more than when bread abounds and wine flows freely.

PSALM 4:7 VOICE

The golden nugget from today's scripture is that God is the one who fills us with joy. It's through faith in Him that we're able to receive the good things He has in store for those who love Him. We are terribly limited by our humanity, which is why we must rely on God to make up the difference. Where we fall short, He fills in the gaps. Where we waver, the Lord strengthens.

This is why we depend on Him every day. This is also why we're able to live with joy and delight, regardless of our struggles. Friend, if you find yourself living a life void of these things, be quick to ask God for help. Share your heart, and tell Him what you need. Don't miss out on the wonderful blessings that come from a trusting relationship with the Lord.

....

....

....

....

....

....

....

....

....

God, fill me with unrivaled joy so I can shine Your goodness into each day with passion and purpose. In Jesus' name. Amen.

Doing What's Right

The hope of those who do right is joy and celebration,
but the only prospect for those who do wrong is futility.
PROVERBS 10:28 VOICE

It's not always easy to do what's right, because so often the right choice is the hardest choice to make. It's difficult to be the lone voice speaking up for truth. It's tough to advocate for those unable to stand up for themselves. It's hard deciding to take a different path when those you love won't follow. But every time you pursue God's leading, He is delighted. It doesn't go unnoticed.

What decisions are you grappling with right now? Are they about your relationships? Do they involve your finances or career? Are they choices about your health? Make no mistake: there is a right and wrong choice facing you right now. Make today a good day by doing the right thing—the thing God is making clear through thoughtful and persistent prayer.

....

....

....

....

....

....

....

....

....

God, impress upon my heart Your plan in the choices I'm
making. I want to know Your desire for my life. I want to
be in Your will every day. In Jesus' name. Amen.

Whose Battle Is It?

Moses spoke to the people: "Don't be afraid. Stand firm and watch
GOD do his work of salvation for you today. Take a good look at the
Egyptians today for you're never going to see them again. GOD will
fight the battle for you. And you? You keep your mouths shut!"
EXODUS 14:13–14 MSG

Sometimes the best plan is to just keep our mouths shut. Amen? Many of us
are quick to respond when we feel pressure from both sides. In our fear, we
try to control the situation ourselves. We try to manage everyone around us.
And while there are times we're called to the battlefield by God, there are other
times we need to step back and let Him fight instead. Bad days happen when
we don't know which option is the right one.

So, friend, be prayerful when difficult situations arise. Before responding,
pray. Take a breath. Maybe even walk away. We don't want to be in the way
when the battle is God's. And we don't want to cause distress or harm by
jumping ahead.

....

....

....

....

....

....

....

....

Dear God, give me the wisdom and discernment to
know whose battle it is. In Jesus' name. Amen.

Rescue Moments

I will shout for joy as I sing Your praises; my soul will
celebrate because You have rescued me.
PSALM 71:23 VOICE

Can you think of times God rescued you? Maybe it was from a toxic and unhealthy relationship. Maybe it was the restoration of a marriage on the brink of divorce. Maybe it was the right job at the right time. Maybe it was a divine download of perfect words in the middle of a hard conversation. Or maybe it was a door of opportunity that closed and the revelation of what God saved you from came later.

The psalmist was so blessed by his rescue that he broke out in shouts and praises. Right there, in the middle of his day, his joy bubbled up as he recognized the Lord's intervention. Don't you think there is something beautiful about a grateful heart? Is your heart grateful? Today, meditate on those rescue moments and celebrate them in God's presence.

....

....

....

....

....

....

....

....

God, I confess the times I've failed to praise You in gratitude.
I can clearly see the times You've rescued me now,
and I want to thank You for being my Savior. You are
a good Father! In Jesus' name. Amen.

The Blessing of Being Overshadowed

But let them all be glad, those who turn aside to hide themselves in you. May they keep shouting for joy forever! Overshadow them in your presence as they sing and rejoice. Then every lover of your name will burst forth with endless joy.
PSALM 5:11 TPT

Can you think of a time you wanted to hide yourself in the Lord? We can sometimes find ourselves stuck in difficult circumstances, longing to be over-shadowed by God's presence. We want to feel sheltered and tucked away. It's in those moments that we find comfort. As believers, God is ready and willing to cover us as we cling to Him.

There's something beautiful that's birthed in us when we feel God's love. It causes praises to erupt from deep inside, even if they manifest as tears and whispers of gratitude on the outside. It allows us to take a breath, inhaling His goodness and exhaling our burdens. And in the end, we're filled with joy to take into each day.

God, I long to be overshadowed by Your presence, especially when I feel exposed. And I am excited that joy will follow. In Jesus' name. Amen.

Heaven Celebrated You

"That's the way God responds every time one lost sinner repents
and turns to him. He says to all his angels, 'Let's have a joyous
celebration, for the one who was lost, I have found!' "
LUKE 15:10 TPT

Have you ever considered that the day you accepted Jesus as your Savior, heaven rejoiced? Ponder how many millions of people are on earth today. To think even one repented soul garners the attention of the heavenly hosts paints a powerful picture of your worth, doesn't it?

Many of us walk around every day feeling worthless. We feel unnoticed or unloved. It's a painful truth that often knits us together as women. Maybe God included today's passage in the Bible specifically to build our confidence. To know our moment of conversion was noticed and celebrated in heaven validates even the weariest soul. So, every time you feel unimportant, remember all of heaven knows who you are.

....

....

....

....

....

....

....

....

God, to know I matter that much to You is a treasured truth I will
carry with me every day. Thank You for drawing me close and
securing my salvation! I love You. In Jesus' name. Amen.

Made for Community

Bless your enemies; no cursing under your breath. Laugh with your happy friends when they're happy; share tears when they're down. Get along with each other; don't be stuck-up. Make friends with nobodies; don't be the great somebody.
ROMANS 12:14–16 MSG

You were made for community. Sometimes our community is easy to love, and sometimes it's not. It can include both your friends and family—and even those you consider enemies. The truth is that God wants us to get along with each other.

Look for opportunities every day to bless those around you. Be kind and generous with your time, talents, and treasure. And always remember you have the power to make someone's day shine. So, whether the task is easy or you need God's help to muster the grace, be the kind of woman who shines the love of Jesus into the lives of others.

....

....

....

....

....

....

....

....

God, give me a heart that sees the good in those around me. Even if they're difficult to love, tender my heart so I am able. Thank You for the gift of community, even though it's messy at times. In Jesus' name. Amen.

Stay Focused on Jesus

Now stay focused on Jesus, who designed and perfected our faith. He endured the cross and ignored the shame of that death because He focused on the joy that was set before Him; and now He is seated beside God on the throne, a place of honor.
HEBREWS 12:2 VOICE

Every day, we face countless distractions that threaten to take our eyes off Jesus. Sometimes we let fear get in the way, and we sink in our worry. We let busyness hijack our priorities, putting other tasks above the Lord. And we get caught up in what this world considers important and never consider God's plan for our day.

What a wonderful reminder for us to stay focused on Jesus! We are fully capable of communing with Him all day long. And if your desire is to have your very best day, that will only happen when you include the Lord. Ask for His guidance. Thank Him for the gift of the cross. And let His awesomeness fill you with joy!

....

....

....

....

....

....

....

....

....

God, I invite You to be part of my every day. I am excited for Your constant companionship! In Jesus' name. Amen.

A Good Life

This is a good life—my heart is glad, my soul is full of joy,
and my body is at rest. Who could want for more?
PSALM 16:9 VOICE

Are you able to say that your life is good? As believers, this is something we can *all* say without fail. It doesn't mean you haven't had hardships and problems. It doesn't mean your life has been a charmed one. And it doesn't mean you've been spared heartache. Chances are you've experienced tragedy and grief and pain at levels of intensity you never thought imaginable. But none of those are disqualifiers for a good life when your faith is in God.

So don't let yourself live each day with a victim mentality. Don't live offended. And stop ruminating about all the terrible things you've faced. The truth is we've all been punched in the gut by life a time or two. Instead, have a glad heart and a joyful soul. Rest in God's peace. And know that when you do, your life will be good!

God, thank You for shifting my perspective today. With You,
my life is a good one! In Jesus' name. Amen.

The Awesomeness of God

All the popular gods are stuff and nonsense, but GOD made the cosmos!
Splendor and majesty flow out of him, strength and joy fill his place.
1 CHRONICLES 16:26–27 MSG

Let's never underestimate the sovereignty and awesomeness of God. Let's remember He is all-powerful, all-mighty, and all-knowing. The Lord is Creator of the heavens and the earth, and He made everything in them. Before you took your first breath, God numbered your days and determined the path for your life. And He has complete understanding of and control over the happenings in the world.

What does this mean for you? It means you can live with confidence. Fear and insecurities and striving aren't the ones in charge. Your faith will direct you to follow God's lead, resting under His love and grace. So, when life feels too big and you feel too small, pray. Let the Lord's splendor and majesty, strength and joy be the reasons for your hope!

....
....
....
....
....
....
....
....

God, I am in awe of You! Forgive me for the times I didn't understand
the height, depth, and width of Your magnificence. Help me live
each day with a faithful confidence. In Jesus' name. Amen.

Making Your Life a Prayer

Let joy be your continual feast. Make your life a prayer.
And in the midst of everything be always giving thanks,
for this is God's perfect plan for you in Christ Jesus.
1 THESSALONIANS 5:16–18 TPT

When the Word tells you to make your life a prayer, it means being intentional to live in community with God. It's deciding to make Him an integral part of your day. . .your week. . .your life. It's choosing to involve Him in the things that matter to you. It's making sure your life reflects your faith in all you say and do. What a beautiful offering to God!

Today, think about ways your life can be a prayer. How can you bless the Lord through it? How can this posture be an encouragement to friends and family? What are the good things you'll receive by living this way each day?

....

....

....

....

....

....

....

....

God, I know Your perfect plan for my life is to be in
relationship with You because by doing so, I will not only
be blessed but also be a blessing. Show me how to make
my life a prayer. In Jesus' name. Amen.

Worthy

The Eternal your God is standing right here among you, and He is the champion who will rescue you. He will joyfully celebrate over you; He will rest in His love for you; He will joyfully sing because of you like a new husband.
ZEPHANIAH 3:17 VOICE

This is one of those verses that touches deep places in your soul. It's a go-to verse when you feel rejected or abandoned by people in your world. It's the passage that tells you you're worthy of being rescued—worthy of being celebrated. When you feel unloved, this is the weighty reminder needed. Take a minute and read it again, friend.

You're *so* important. You are *so* loved and valued. And you can choose to stand strong in this verse every day, no matter what. Nothing and no one can take this truth from you. So, if you're looking for ways to live your best life, let this declaration be the foundation.

....

....

....

....

....

....

....

....

God, what a blessing to have Your Word to speak into my weary soul. Help me find my worth in its pages rather than looking to the world for validation. I know the world is an empty well. In Jesus' name. Amen.

God Is Pleased

So here is what you should do: go and enjoy your meals, drink your wine and love every minute of it because God is already pleased with what you do.

God doesn't want you to live your life worried about what He thinks about you. He doesn't want you stressed out, wondering if He's pleased with you. Because you are His child, God sees you through the blood of Jesus. Your sins are washed away—past, present, and future—and you're white as snow.

Remember the goal of godly living is not being perfect. In our humanity, it's completely unattainable. Instead, the goal is choosing to live with purpose. It's having passion for the Lord demonstrated through your life. But know if you're walking out your faith every day, God is delighted. When you spend time in prayer, He's smiling. And every time you open the Word, it fills His heart with joy.

....

....

....

....

....

....

....

....

God, help me remember Your love is not conditional or performance based. The world has conditioned me to think otherwise, but that is not who You are. I'm grateful You see me through the blood of Jesus. In His name. Amen.

Never Alone

In the day of trouble, he will treasure me in his shelter,
under the cover of his tent. He will lift me high upon a rock,
out of reach from all my enemies who surround me.
PSALM 27:5 TPT

Even on the worst days, God is there for you. He is with you. Scripture says He'll shelter you and cover you. God will lift you up so you're out of reach from those who want to hurt you. As a believer, you're never left alone to figure things out by yourself. What a relief!

So, when the day of trouble comes, fear not. Don't let worry take over. There's no need to feel helpless. You are in God's hands, *always*. And that is the very best place to be! So, friend, on that day, stand in victory. It may not make the pain and hardship go away, but it will settle your heart as you feel surrounded by the Lord's mighty presence.

....

....

....

....

....

....

....

....

God, thank You for never leaving me to my own devices. In good times or very challenging times, I know You'll be there to help. I'm never alone. In Jesus' name. Amen.

When They Don't Like You

God lifts me high above those with thoughts of death and deceit that call for my life. I will enter His presence, offering sacrifices and praise. In His house, I am overcome with joy as I sing, yes, and play music for the Eternal alone.
PSALM 27:6 VOICE

Even if you are the kindest woman on the planet, there will be people who don't like you. It doesn't matter how generous you are with your time, talent, or treasure, someone will find you annoying. Because when you stand in truth and speak about your faith, it will be offensive to some.

Don't let it ruin your day. That may be easy to say, but God is ready to still your spirit in that moment. Go right into prayer; ask Him to replace your heartache with joy. Praise Him in advance, believing He'll follow through on His promise to protect you. Let God overwhelm you with His love so your mood stays light and loving.

....

....

....

....

....

....

....

....

....

God, I don't want haters to have power over my day or dampen my spirit. Lift me above it so my spirit soars with You instead! In Jesus' name. Amen.

The Problem of Busy Thoughts

Whenever my busy thoughts were out of control, the soothing comfort of your presence calmed me down and overwhelmed me with delight.

PSALM 94:19 TPT

We all know the overwhelming feeling that floods our hearts when thoughts run rampant. Left unchecked, we begin to partner with lies. These untruths create havoc, causing deep worry and anxiety. We get stressed out. And before we know it, we're in a full-blown panic. Our mood is shot; our productivity is down the drain; and our day is ruined.

God invites us to come to Him in these messy moments. He understands the complexity of our emotions and how they've been affected by our busy thoughts. And when we do, our anxious hearts will find comfort. Scripture says we'll be overwhelmed by a sense of joy. So, friend, let God be the one to help you get your day back on track.

....

....

....

....

....

....

....

God, help me keep my thoughts trained on Your goodness rather than worldly things that cause fear and worry. And if I do get tangled up in them, remind me You're the great detangler. I don't want anything to ruin this glorious day! In Jesus' name. Amen.

A Glorious Habit

So here's what I've learned through it all: Leave all your cares and anxieties at the feet of the Lord, and measureless grace will strengthen you.
PSALM 55:22 TPT

When you offload the burdens you're carrying and leave them at the feet of the Lord, you'll feel the weight of them lift. God has offered to take them from you at any time, leaving you unhindered and free. Why not let Him figure everything out?

As you lay your head down to sleep, tell the Lord every care and anxious thought. From the big burdens to the small annoyances, give them all to Him. And in the morning, watch as you wake up lighter. You're set up for a wonderful day fueled by God's grace and strength. Friend, let this become your glorious habit in faith.

....

....

....

....

....

....

....

....

God, help me leave my cares and anxieties with You each night so my mornings are full of joy and peace. Let me trust that You're working all things out in my favor so I'm no longer burdened with trying to figure everything out on my own. Thank You for taking care of me! In Jesus' name. Amen.

Your Battle Plan

Here's what I've learned through it all: Don't give up; don't be impatient;
be entwined as one with the Lord. Be brave and courageous, and never
lose hope. Yes, keep on waiting—for he will never disappoint you!
PSALM 27:14 TPT

Let this verse be your battle plan when things begin to go south. Understand that problems will come your way. Every day, there's a good chance something will threaten your peace. But as the psalmist says in today's verse, don't give up. Don't be impatient as you wait for God to intervene. Instead, wrap yourself up in the Lord.

Why? Because doing so builds confidence that He will be the hero in your story. It emboldens you to stand strong through every kind of test and trial. And it makes you remember all the times God has come through for you. Life is full of disappointments, but God will never be one of them.

....

....

....

....

....

....

....

....

....

God, help me trust You as I wait for Your hand to move. Make me
bold. Give me courage. Fill me with endless hope. You're why I can
have a good day today and every day! In Jesus' name. Amen.

The Path of Pain

See if there is any path of pain I'm walking on, and lead me back to your
glorious, everlasting way—the path that brings me back to you.
PSALM 139:24 TPT

There are times we sit in our pain too long. When we do, it can interrupt our day, mess with our week, and if left alone, it can destroy our life. The truth is that pain and grief deserve their time. God created us with a full range of emotions, and they are ours to feel. But if we're walking on a path of pain without God, we may never change directions.

Let the Lord, at the right time, lead you back to the path planned for your life. We need His intervention to stay the course without looking to the left or the right. The Lord is the great course corrector, so follow His lead. He's the one who will ensure a good day by keeping you walking in the right direction.

....

....

....

....

....

....

....

....

....

....

God, be quick to lead me back to Your glorious and
everlasting way so I am close to You and not stuck trying
to nurse my pain. In Jesus' name. Amen.

A Breakthrough Season

Let my passion for life be restored, tasting joy in every breakthrough you bring to me. Hold me close to you with a willing spirit that obeys whatever you say.

PSALM 51:12 TPT

Have you lost your passion for life? Has every day become dull and joyless? Honestly, it makes sense. Life is hard and grueling. We read bad news in the headlines and watch sad stories unfold on the news. We struggle with our finances and our health and our relationships. And so often, the daily grind wears us down and we feel broken.

But friend, let today be the start of a breakthrough season. Choose to tell God about all the things burdening your heart right now. He may know every detail, but your obedience to confess starts the process of healing. There is joy waiting for you on the other side! Let God hold you close as He restores your passion every day.

....

....

....

....

....

....

....

....

....

God, please be gracious and restore my joy for life. Give me a divine breakthrough so I can embrace the plan You've determined for my life with passion and purpose daily. In Jesus' name. Amen.

Bold Prayers

God, I invite your searching gaze into my heart. Examine me through
and through; find out everything that may be hidden within me.
Put me to the test and sift through all my anxious cares.

PSALM 139:23 TPT

This is a very bold prayer! It's a prayer prayed by one ready to mature in his faith. He wants everything hidden to be found. The desire is for God to dig deep in his heart to reveal and heal what's broken. The psalmist wants anything that threatens to hinder their relationship exposed. And friend, this should be our prayer too.

If we want to grow our faith, then let's be willing to invite God to this level of examination. He has a perfect track record in our lives, reminding us we can trust Him to handle everything with care. God won't be reckless with our hearts. And this act of surrender will lighten our hearts and brighten our days!

....

....

....

....

....

....

....

....

....

God, You are invited to examine my heart through and through.
Find and free me from any anxious cares that keep me from living
in the freedom Jesus came to bring. In Jesus' name. Amen.

Gratitude for the Creator

I thank you, God, for making me so mysteriously complex!
Everything you do is marvelously breathtaking. It simply amazes
me to think about it! How thoroughly you know me, Lord!
PSALM 139:14 TPT

As women, it's hard to imagine having enough confidence to be in awe of ourselves. Not necessarily in a prideful way but just choosing to embrace the complexity of who we are in a positive light. We're often so quick to cut ourselves down or disqualify ourselves from compliments. But have you ever considered how that makes God feel? If we are His creation and constantly dogging how we're made, how does that honor Him?

Start each day with a heart of gratitude for God the Creator. Thank Him for who He made you to be, even if you're insecure about it. Acknowledge His eye for detail and careful thoughtfulness. Celebrate His meticulous and contemplative design. And watch how it changes the way you feel about yourself.

....

....

....

....

....

....

....

....

God, forgive me for discounting Your creation. And help
me be more grateful, knowing how thoroughly You know
me, because You made me. In Jesus' name. Amen.

Where Are Your Eyes?

"Step out of the traffic! Take a long, loving look at me,
your High God, above politics, above everything."
PSALM 46:10 MSG

What a timely reminder! In a world that feels like it's gone crazy—with every-body fighting about race, religion, politics, and everything in between—let this verse guide your next step. And consider that it may be moving in a fresh direction, one with your eyes directly on God alone. When you're destabilized, God is the one who settles your spirit.

Even with the craziness, you can walk through each day with a powerful peace. The mood for your day isn't dependent on the mood of the nation. You can find joy in the hardest of seasons. As a matter of fact, God may be asking you to shine a light of hope to those around you right now. And that's only something you can do when your eyes are on God above all else.

....

....

....

....

....

....

....

....

....

God, help me fix my gaze on Your face when I'm anxious about
life. Anchor me to You so the chaos of the world doesn't breech
the peace in my heart. In Jesus' name. Amen.

Refuge

He who takes refuge in the shelter of the Most High
will be safe in the shadow of the Almighty.
PSALM 91:1 VOICE

Where do you look for refuge? Your husband? Your parents? Is it in retail therapy or a box of cookies? Is it hiding in bed, bingeing your favorite Netflix show? Is it escaping through your favorite game on your phone or a fantasy novel that transports you to another universe? Or maybe it's consuming the wrong things in excess. The truth is, we all have something we consider our go-to solution. And, as many have discovered, any comfort is short-lived and empty.

Every day you can walk in victory by letting God be your refuge. In His shelter, you'll find a place of rest. His shadow will block the enemy's plans to hurt you. God's presence is the safest place for you to release emotions and let your heart heal. So be quick to go to the Lord first. There is no better place to be.

....

....

....

....

....

....

....

....

....

....

God, there is no substitute for the shelter You provide to those
who love You. And I love You! In Jesus' name. Amen.

Keep Creating

Keep creating in me a clean heart. Fill me with pure
thoughts and holy desires, ready to please you.
PSALM 51:10 TPT

When the writer asks God for help, he knows he's asking for a continual process. Notice he didn't use the word *create*, but rather the words *keep creating*. It's ongoing, daily work that requires constant monitoring and fixing by the Father's hand. And it's an act of love that God is willing to care for us in such a way.

"Keep creating"—let this be your request to God every day. It's brilliant to ask Him to fill us with pure thoughts and holy desires, because our minds are a battlefield every day. And honestly, it doesn't take much for us to release our thoughts to go their own direction. It's our heart that drives them. So asking God to keep your heart clean helps ensure your thoughts follow suit. Ask God to purify and renew you every morning. What better way to start the day!

....

....

....

....

....

....

....

....

....

God, keep my mind and thoughts above reproach by actively and
continually purifying them. Let me think of noble and godly things—
things that glorify Your holiness! In Jesus' name. Amen.

Coming Gifts

Take great joy in the Eternal! His gifts are coming,
and they are all your heart desires!
PSALM 37:4 VOICE

Don't misinterpret today's scripture. When the Bible tells us we will get our heart's desires, it's assumed our desires are aligned with God's desires for us. Every day, we should be deepening our faith by digging into the Word to learn more about our Father. We should pray, seeking His will for our lives. And our focus should be on glorifying Him with our words and actions.

Once those are taking place, God's *coming gifts* for us will delight our hearts because they delight His. We may not have a bigger house, but we will have a bigger heart full of compassion. We may not have fame, but we will spread God's name near and far. We may not have an easy life, but we'll have a testimony full of God's goodness to share. These are priceless gifts to any believer. And, in faith, they are coming.

....

....

....

....

....

....

....

....

God, help my heart's desires align with Yours. Let my
focus be on pleasing You rather than storing up
treasures on earth for me. In Jesus' name. Amen.

Struggle to Trust

You who sit down in the High God's presence, spend the night in Shaddai's shadow, say this: "GOD, you're my refuge. I trust in you and I'm safe!"

PSALM 91:1–2 MSG

Trust is tricky. For many, it's a sticking point in our relationships. It's not that we don't want to trust those we love; we're just scared of getting hurt again. We're afraid of being let down once more. It feels as if our hearts can't handle one more ounce of pain that comes from betrayal, rejection, or abandonment. Sometimes, that's exactly why we struggle to trust God.

Let today mark a change in your mindset. If there is anyone to trust, it's the Lord. Looking back on your life, you'd see God's unwavering faithfulness in every single one of your circumstances. You'd find His trustworthiness in every struggle. Friend, there's great freedom in letting God be your refuge and safe place. And when it feels impossible, ask Him to give you confidence and courage to trust Him once again.

God, I need You, but I'm afraid to trust again. Penetrate my heart with Your love so I can. In Jesus' name. Amen.

What Do You Crave Most?

*Here's the one thing I crave from Yahweh, the one thing I seek
above all else: I want to live with him every moment in his house,
beholding the marvelous beauty of Yahweh, filled with awe, delighting
in his glory and grace. I want to contemplate in his temple.*

What are the things you enjoy in life? What do you crave from the world? Maybe fulfilling relationships and faithful friends? Good health and enough money to pay the bills? Traveling the world and seeing new places? Others may want fame and fortune and everything in between. They collect earthly treasures and toys, as well as the finer things in life. But unless we're craving the presence of God and eternity in heaven *more* than everything else, we need to revisit our priorities.

God created this world for us to enjoy. But it should never have more of our hearts than heaven. Take inventory of this today. Let God open your eyes to the truth, and make whatever changes are necessary.

....

....

....

....

....

....

....

....

....

*God, show me where my heart is on this. I want my time with You
in eternity to be my greatest longing. In Jesus' name. Amen.*

Giving Up Control

Commit your path to the Eternal; let Him direct you. Put your confidence in Him, and He will follow through with you.
PSALM 37:5 VOICE

It's hard to let someone else determine our daily path. Why? Because we're women, and we have well-thought-out plans! We're pros at being organized and epic at keeping a schedule. We can multitask with the best of them, tying up all loose ends with ease. And to suggest we hand our calendar over to another feels. . .well, silly. Things are easier when we run the show, amen?

But as faith-filled believers, following God's lead is vital. And truthfully, there's endless freedom in it. Who knew giving up control and trusting the Lord with the details would bring such joy? Scripture clearly says we can be confident because He will follow through! So today, invite Him to lead, and enjoy the break!

....
....
....
....
....
....
....
....

God, this is challenging for me because I am the one who manages my home. I'm used to being the daily decision-maker. But I want to follow Your Word, so You're glorified. Help me release control and follow You. Let it be an adventure! In Jesus' name. Amen.

With the Right Attitude

Instead you thrill to God's Word, you chew on Scripture day and night. You're a tree replanted in Eden, bearing fresh fruit every month, never dropping a leaf, always in blossom.
PSALM 1:2–3 MSG

There's a blessing that comes from time in God's Word with the right attitude. When we approach scripture with expectation and excitement, it will bring much-needed nourishment. Our weary souls will drink in its goodness, and fruit will be produced in abundance. But so often, we open the Bible with a legalistic focus. We think we must read the Bible, so we rush through the verses, gleaning little, if anything. And it becomes nothing more than a line on our to-do list we can check off each day.

Let today's verses challenge you to change things up! Have a reverent heart as you grab your Bible and open its pages. Begin reading, knowing God will speak. Open your heart to hear new things in fresh ways. Talk to God through it. Ask Him questions. Share your thoughts. Meditate and pray. And when you take this position, you'll come alive like a tree in full bloom.

....

....

....

....

....

....

....

....

God, teach me to love Your Word. In Jesus' name. Amen.

Wide-Open Field

But me he caught—reached all the way from sky to sea; he pulled me out
of that ocean of hate, that enemy chaos, the void in which I was drowning.
They hit me when I was down, but GOD stuck by me. He stood me up
on a wide-open field; I stood there saved—surprised to be loved!
PSALM 18:16–19 MSG

Let the visual in today's verses be healing salve for your weary heart. To know God sees you from His heavenly throne and reaches down to pull you to Him is a beautiful image of His love. No matter what's threatening to pull you under, God goes right in after you, unafraid. You may feel abandoned momentarily, left alone in the mess. But your Father is with you *right now*.

You can feel relief today, friend. Let God rescue you. Let Him place you in a wide-open field where you're free. No more crushing pressure from others' agendas. No expectations. No criticism. When you cry out to Him, God will free you to live your best days surrounded by His love and protection.

God, help me. In Jesus' name. Amen.

Bringing Honor to God's Name

That's where he restores and revives my life. He opens before
me the right path and leads me along in his footsteps of
righteousness so that I can bring honor to his name.
PSALM 23:3 TPT

Consider that maybe your grand purpose in life is to bring honor to God's name—not that He requires it or needs it. Not that the responsibility of it rests on your shoulders. Not that you're the chosen one (even though you're pretty awesome). But recognize that God's plan to share the gospel with the world is through His believers. And while we're imperfect at best, choosing to live righteously impacts others.

Every day is another opportunity to bring Him honor. Look for ways to be His hands and feet. Live unoffended and full of joy. Be honest about your walk with God, ready to share your testimony of His goodness. And live with confidence so others see His strength and wisdom flowing through you. That's how you honor God's name.

God, what a privilege to point others to You with my
life. Let me be mindful of my words and actions so
You're glorified. In Jesus' name. Amen.

When You Want a Best Friend

Yahweh is my best friend and my shepherd.
I always have more than enough.
PSALM 23:1 TPT

Were you one of the girls who always craved a best friend but never found one? You longed for that special person to be silly with. You prayed for a bestie to hang out with. In your mind, having that one friend would make life so much better. And, while you had good friends, your heart's desire eluded you.

The psalmist found that kind of special friendship with God. No more waiting or begging for companionship because the Lord filled that void for him. You know what? God can be your best friend too. He fits all the criteria. He's there anytime you need Him. There's nothing you can't share with Him. He will always have your back. And He wants what's best for you. So perk up! Your best friend is here!

....

....

....

....

....

....

....

God, You really do think of everything. I've hoped and wished for a bestie as far back as I can remember, but it never happened. I'm grateful You'll be that for me! When I forget, remind me You're right there anytime and every time. In Jesus' name. Amen.

The Valley of the Deepest Darkness

Even when your path takes me through the valley of deepest darkness, fear will never conquer me, for you already have! Your authority is my strength and my peace. The comfort of your love takes away my fear. I'll never be lonely, for you are near.

PSALM 23:4 TPT

When we find ourselves in the valley of the deepest darkness and when fear feels overwhelming because of the unknowns ahead, God's love brings lasting comfort. His strength keeps us moving forward. And it's the Lord's peace that settles our spirit. Let's remember we're never alone in those times. God is right there, walking with us, guiding us, and caring for our needs.

So, friend, when your days are marked by valley moments, cling to the Lord with all your might. He's leading you through for your good and His glory, and He is trustworthy! Even when you find yourself surrounded by darkness, God will be your light.

....

....

....

....

....

....

....

God, thank You that even hard days can be good days when we hold on to You. Guide me through them with strength, peace, and the comfort of Your love. In Jesus' name. Amen.

Staying Present in Today

So why would I fear the future? Only goodness and tender love pursue
me all the days of my life. Then afterward, when my life is through,
I'll return to your glorious presence to be forever with you!
PSALM 23:6 TPT

Sometimes we get a little ahead of ourselves. Rather than stay present in today, navigating the ups and downs that come with it, we begin to worry about tomorrow. Many of us see only terrible outcomes and endings as we look into the future. We become overwhelmed by the countless unknowns down the road. And it ruins our day.

When we project like that, we're taking God out of the picture. We're forgetting He's already in our tomorrows. He goes before us. God's goodness and favor follow us. And no matter what it brings, we're secured by His tender love. Stand strong in today and enjoy its blessings. Tomorrow can wait.

....

....

....

....

....

....

....

....

....

God, I love the gentle reminder to not fear the future. Help me stay
present in today so I can embrace all You have in store for me.
I trust You with what's ahead. In Jesus' name. Amen.

Every Need You Have

Know this: my God will also fill every need you have according to
His glorious riches in Jesus the Anointed, our Liberating King.
PHILIPPIANS 4:19 VOICE

If God says He'll meet your need, then He *will* meet your need. It's as simple as that. And maybe it's not hard to believe when you stand in faith. But here's where we get messed up: our fear comes into play because we're not sure God will answer our prayers in the way we want them answered. We worry He won't meet our needs how we want them met. Amen?

Our challenge is to believe that not only is God trustworthy in our circumstances but also that His plans are always for our good and His glory. Scripture is clear that the Lord will fill every need you have. Once you share your heart, your job is to stand in faith knowing God will come through in ways that will delight.

....

....

....

....

....

....

....

....

God, whatever Your plans are for me, I will be grateful. I'm choosing to
embrace Your generosity and kindness, even if it's not what I expected.
You are always good, and I am thankful! In Jesus' name. Amen.

Running from Immorality

Run from immoral behavior. All other sins are disconnected from the body, but sexual immorality is a sin against your own body. Don't you know that your body is the temple of the Holy Spirit who comes from God and dwells inside of you? You do not own yourself.

1 CORINTHIANS 6:18–19 VOICE

If God's Word tells you to run from immoral behavior, then you may need to pick up the pace. Friend, your best day starts with pursuing a life of purity. It's called righteous living, which is exactly what the Lord is asking for.

God's hope for you is to recognize your body as His Holy Spirit's temple. It's sacred because He is sacred. When you allow sexual sin in any form, the Word says you're sinning against that temple—your body. Commit to purity each day, and watch how your faith flourishes. Choose the path that gives you peace.

....

....

....

....

....

....

....

....

....

God, help me stay focused on keeping my body holy. Protect me from anything that might cause me to stumble into sexual immorality. And thank You for the Holy Spirit's presence in me. In Jesus' name. Amen.

God Will Take Care of It

Don't hit back; discover beauty in everyone. If you've got it in you,
get along with everybody. Don't insist on getting even; that's not for
you to do. "I'll do the judging," says God. "I'll take care of it."
ROMANS 12:19 MSG

Sometimes we want to exact revenge on those who've hurt us. Because our love is fierce for our loved ones, we're ready to defend them at all costs. We think it'll give us pleasure to see someone pay. God, however, isn't on board with our plan. Instead, He promises to take care of it for us. He'll be the one to judge.

Be quick to pray when those revenge feelings start bubbling to the surface. Let God know your thoughts and fears and worries. Tell Him about your heartache and anger. When you surrender these to Him, it will keep your heart from becoming hard. Then you'll be free to discover the goodness of others. And *that* will make for a glorious life.

....

....

....

....

....

....

....

....

....

God, remind me again that You'll defend me and right all
the wrongs. Help me keep a loving heart as I trust You
to take care of it all. In Jesus' name. Amen.

Slow to Anger

My dearest brothers and sisters, take this to heart: Be quick to listen,
but slow to speak. And be slow to become angry, for human anger
is never a legitimate tool to promote God's righteous purpose.
JAMES 1:19–20 TPT

Few things can ruin a day faster than anger. It has a way of derailing the best of times by stirring up old wounds. It reminds you of past offenses, bringing back memories of painful moments. Even more, if people know you're a believer, it can ruin your testimony of faith.

Instead of jumping to irritation, God's Word tells us to listen first. Let others share their heart—including their hurts. Stay quiet so they feel heard. And then ask God for compassion and understanding. Doing so validates their pain and allows you to remain calm. Every day is a chance to love others well. Let's choose to walk this verse out so God gets all the glory.

....
....
....
....
....
....
....
....

God, sometimes my temper flares without warning.
Forgive me for the times I've not honored You with my words
and actions. I confess I've treated others unjustly. Help
me be ready to listen first. In Jesus' name. Amen.

When Your Joy Is from Jesus

Express your joy; be happy in Him, you who are good and true. Go ahead, shout and rejoice aloud, you whose hearts are honest and straightforward.
PSALM 32:11 VOICE

Don't you love hanging out with joyful people? No matter what you're going through, they lift your spirit. They help take your mind off the heaviness in your life and put a smile on your face. You may even envy their positive outlook on life, especially knowing their world is messy and hard. And when their joy is fueled by their relationship with God, it's a powerful force.

Friend, this is available to you too! Happiness in Jesus doesn't mean your life is perfect. It doesn't negate the stress and strife you face. But it does allow you to rise above the circumstances because your eyes are firmly fixed on His goodness. Joy doesn't happen because of perfection. Joy happens because of Jesus.

....

....

....

....

....

....

....

....

....

God, help me find joy and happiness through my relationship with You. There will be seasons when life is hard, but that doesn't have to affect my joyfulness. In Jesus' name. Amen.

God Hears Your Prayers

Blessed be GOD—he heard me praying. He proved he's on my side; I've thrown my lot in with him. Now I'm jumping for joy, and shouting and singing my thanks to him.
PSALM 28:6–7 MSG

God hears you. When you cry out to Him, scripture confirms over and over again that your voice is heard. It doesn't matter the time of day or if it's a holiday, God is never off-duty. He isn't preoccupied with other situations. You aren't a low-priority prayer. What a relief!

This means that all day long, you can talk to God. Your conversation can start once your eyes open in the morning and last until you drift off to sleep. Be it traffic on the way to work, patience with a friend at lunch, or preparing dinner, God can be part of it all because He hears you pray. And it delights His heart to be in that kind of community with you.

....
....
....
....
....
....
....
....
....

God, my heart is full when I realize You're always available to me. Thank You for being accessible to me and interested in me. In Jesus' name. Amen.

Telling God Your Needs

*I'm letting you know what I need, calling out for help and
lifting my arms toward your inner sanctuary.*
PSALM 28:2 MSG

The best person to share your needs with is God. He has a vested interest in your life because He's the one who created you. As a matter of fact, God knows your needs before you do. He understands the complexity of your emotions. He knows where the deficits in your life lie. The Lord understands where you fall short and what gaps need to be filled.

Don't waste a minute of your day trying to be brave and figure things out on your own. Don't wallow in self-pity. And don't look to anyone else to fix your circumstances. Go directly to God, and let Him sort it out. He will either empower you, call in the troops, or handle it Himself. Regardless, you're in good hands when you let God be God.

....

....

....

....

....

....

....

....

....

*God, hear my voice, and see my position of surrender. My heart is
heavy, and I cannot do this without You. Let me feel the peace that
comes from Your presence right now. In Jesus' name. Amen.*

Sowing and Reaping

Those who sow their tears as seeds will reap a harvest with joyful shouts of glee. They may weep as they go out carrying their seed to sow, but they will return with joyful laughter and shouting with gladness as they bring back armloads of blessing and a harvest overflowing!
PSALM 126:5–6 TPT

Do you know believers who are sad all the time, overwhelmed by life, and hopeless? There's no joy or happiness. They play victim or martyr, wearing it like a crown. Friend, Jesus didn't die for you or me to live a life in this kind of bondage.

Take every tear to the cross. Every hurt or hang up? . . . Give it to the Lord. When you're worried or stressed or insecure, talk to God about what you're feeling. When you continue to sow into your faith, you will reap a beautiful harvest of God's goodness. Just like everyone else, you will have hard days and tough seasons; but when you activate your faith and trust God through the difficult times, He will reward your obedience with joy and gladness. Your harvest of blessings will overflow!

God, let my faithful sowing reap every good thing! In Jesus' name. Amen.

Pain into Joy

You did it: You turned my deepest pains into joyful dancing;
You stripped off my dark clothing and covered me with joyful light.
PSALM 30:11 VOICE

You are a child of the Most High God. There is no reason for you to spend the day drowning in your deepest pain when He is your Father. Don't walk around sulking, covered in shame. Don't partner with guilt. Don't play the victim card. You can have your best day today if you talk to God about the burdens weighing on your heart. There are no perfect words He's waiting to hear. Instead, cry it out; shout it out; let it *all* out. He can handle it.

God has a supernatural way of relieving you of the heaviness that comes with pain. The hurt may not go away, but you will have a peace and comfort that can't be explained by the world. And even in the middle of your junk, you can find overflowing joy. God will literally turn a light on in your heart, and you will see hope. Don't give any day away to pain. Give it to God instead.

....

....

....

....

....

....

....

....

....

God, hear my heart, take my pain, and give
me joy! In Jesus' name. Amen.

Another Chance

Eternal One, my True God, I cried out to You for help; You mended the shattered pieces of my life. You lifted me from the grave with a mighty hand, gave me another chance, and saved me from joining those in that dreadful pit.

PSALM 30:2–3 VOICE

One of the most beautiful truths we are blessed to enjoy as believers is knowing we always get another chance. While many times second chances run out with family and friends, they never do with God. Every mess-up is an opportunity for His grace to shine into our repentant heart. We will never get to the bottom of the jar of chances with God.

Today, thank God for His patience, love, and grace. Thank Him for having no expectation of perfection so we can be free from guilt and shame. And tell the Lord how grateful you are Jesus' blood has washed you clean of every sin—past, present, and future.

....

....

....

....

....

....

....

....

God, I'm full of gratitude when I realize I'm never out of chances. I can cry out to You, and You will mend the shattered pieces of my life. You'll save me from the pit. Thank You. In Jesus' name. Amen.

Letting Him Go Before You

Let your love and steadfast kindness overshadow us
continually, for we trust and we wait upon you!
PSALM 33:22 TPT

We're taught to not be overshadowed. As children, many of us learned to fight for the spotlight. To be seen. To be recognized. We fought to be number one, most popular, and life of the party. If it's not something we learned from our parents, then it was the common message of the world whispered in our ear from a young age. But, as our faith matures, we realize how exposed we are if—and when—we stand ahead of everyone else.

Truly the safest place to be is under God's covering. We can be overshadowed by His love and kindness. By His compassion, His protection, His forgiveness, His restoration, and healing. When you have the proper perspective, you realize the safety of letting God go before you, giving Him that often-coveted position of number one. Today, let's all rejoice because He goes before us! What a blessing to be number two!

....

....

....

....

....

....

....

God, thank You for being number one instead of me and for overshadowing
me in every way! Keep me from stepping outside of Your covering. I
will choose to stay safely tucked in behind. In Jesus' name. Amen.

The Awesomeness of God's Word

For God's Word is something to sing about! He is true
to his promises, his word can be trusted,
and everything he does is reliable and right.
PSALM 33:4 TPT

There are few things you can trust in the world, and God's Word is one of them. What was penned thousands of years ago is still relevant today. It lacks nothing. There are no additions or updates necessary. And 100 percent of the Word is accurate and true. The Bible is alive and active, able to convict and encourage at the same time. And it offers the unique perspective of our heavenly Father. It's God's love letter to us—a powerful way to reveal Himself to those who love Him.

Let God's Word be part of your every day. In all its glory, let the truths throughout its pages penetrate your heart. Let them guide your next step. Meditate on the words, asking God for clarity and insight.

....

....

....

....

....

....

....

God, thank You for the beauty and power of Your written Word.
Let it be important to me and something I carve out time to
invest my heart in daily. In Jesus' name. Amen.

God's Wraparound Presence

The Lord alone is our radiant hope and we trust in him with all
our hearts. His wraparound presence will strengthen us.
PSALM 33:20 TPT

How would your day be different if, in the middle of your mess, you envisioned the very presence of God wrapped around you? It would make for your very best day, wouldn't it? Well, friend, let that be your reality every single day. Ask for it. Let God know you're desperate for a manifestation of His goodness.

It's God's presence that strengthens us for all the ups and downs coming our way. He is why we can have hope of victory and healing and restoration. We don't have to walk around defeated, downcast about our circumstances. God has proven His trustworthiness time and time again, and that gives us confidence He'll intercede as before. So chin up, friend. God is fully present in all of today, wrapping you up in His love and protection!

....

....

....

....

....

....

....

....

Lord, let me feel Your peace right now. Calm my anxious heart from
beating out of my chest. Once again, I'm asking for Your wraparound
presence to cover me in comfort. In Jesus' name. Amen.

Modeling Faith

You paid careful attention to the way we lived among you, and determined to live that way yourselves. In imitating us, you imitated the Master.
1 Thessalonians 1:5 MSG

Friend, every day you have the privilege and burden of modeling faith to those around you. Don't brush it off. Instead, choose to be a godly ambassador. Let the way you live speak volumes. Let your love and compassion point others to God. And always keep in mind that you're being watched, especially when others know you're a believer. This shouldn't intimidate you but rather encourage you to boldly live your faith.

As you take inventory, what are some things you need to change? Where do you need to be more thoughtful? Ask God to show you anything in your life that needs refining, so you'll live a life worthy of imitating. Remember this is not about perfection but about living a life with purpose and passion for God every day.

God, it's an honor to think anything in my life could be worth imitating. Let every word and every action show others Your glory! In Jesus' name. Amen.

Spiritual Refining

Friends, when life gets really difficult, don't jump to the conclusion that God isn't on the job. Instead, be glad that you are in the very thick of what Christ experienced. This is a spiritual refining process, with glory just around the corner.
1 PETER 4:12–13 MSG

It should bring comfort to your heart to know that difficult times are indicative of spiritual refining. Simply put, God does not waste heartache. Instead, He uses it all—every bit. And it's always for your good and His glory. And while it may feel like we're navigating life's challenges alone, scripture is clear that God is not taking a break.

Today, no matter what you're facing, move forward with an attitude of worship. Start right now—praising Him in advance of all the wonderful things He's *going* to do, all the wonderful things He *is doing*. And remember, glory is just around the corner, and faith is the ticket.

....

....

....

....

....

....

....

....

God, I'm thankful You use every struggle and challenge I face for my good. Thank You that it all serves a purpose..Help me keep this perspective, especially when I'm overwhelmed. In Jesus' name. Amen.

Doing Hard Things

So if you find life difficult because you're doing what God said, take it in stride. Trust him. He knows what he's doing, and he'll keep on doing it.
1 PETER 4:19 MSG

The truth is that God asks us to do hard things. Many times, what He wants from those who love Him feels scary. It feels as if we're having to go against the grain, knowing it puts us in unpopular positions. We're called to speak up when we'd rather stay silent. And sometimes, God asks us to stand up to injustices on the behalf of others.

Even when you're asked to step out of your comfort zone, it can be a good day because you can fully trust God. Doing His will shouldn't hang a dark cloud over your plans. As a matter of fact, it often invigorates as you feel His delight over your obedience. So be ready and willing to follow the Lord's prompting. God knows exactly what He's doing *all the time.*

....

....

....

....

....

....

....

....

God, what a privilege to be used by You! Help me trust Your perfect plans so I am confident to step out in obedience. In Jesus' name. Amen.

Even in the Turbulence

I am completely confident and incredibly proud of you. Even in all
this turbulence I am at peace—I am overflowing with joy.
2 CORINTHIANS 7:4 VOICE

It is possible to experience peace in the turbulence of life. Everything may be falling apart around you. Maybe your relationships are in the middle of deep challenges. Maybe your finances are on the verge of destruction. Is your health failing at every turn, or is there a cloud of grief and sadness hanging over you that won't lift? Well, guess what. . .These struggles can't take your peace or joy if you hold on to God through them.

The problem is we often don't. Instead, we try to fix our lives by ourselves. We try to manage every circumstance and person involved so we can steer to a certain outcome. Rather than let God be God, we grab onto the wheel and drive in the direction we feel is best. Friend, regardless of what today brings, staying close to the Lord can make it a good day! Share your heart, and then let Him fill you with His peace and joy.

....

....

....

....

....

....

....

....

....

God, calm my anxious heart. In Jesus' name. Amen.

Owning Up

But if we own up to our sins, God shows that He is faithful and just by forgiving us of our sins and purifying us from the pollution of all the bad things we have done.

1 JOHN 1:9 VOICE

You don't have to carry the guilt and weight of your sins into your day. There's no reason to drag your heavy burdens along with you, because God offers a clear path to freedom. As a believer, why would you choose to hold on to the pollution of sin when God promises to purify you from it?

This is the reason we should be quick to confess our sins. It's important we take responsibility, understanding God isn't expecting perfection from us. We don't have to hide our sin because He knows it all anyway. And if we want each day to be the very best it can be, then let's own up to our trespasses. In a spirit of honesty, admit them to God so you can feel cleansed of all wrongdoing. Then enjoy life to the fullest!

....

....

....

....

....

....

....

....

....

....

God, I confess I am a sinner. Restore me so I can live free of sin's pollution! In Jesus' name. Amen.

Worship Is a Privilege

*Worship Yahweh with gladness. Sing your way into his presence
with joy! And realize what this really means—we have the
privilege of worshiping Yahweh our God. For he is our Creator
and we belong to him. We are the people of his pleasure.*

PSALM 100:2–3 TPT

Have you considered that worshiping God is a privilege? So often we sing in church because that's just what we do. There may not be much heartfelt meaning behind it. We're just following the format of the service. And when good news comes our way, we might say, "Praise the Lord," with a sigh of relief, but do we really understand what we're saying?

This passage of scripture is a challenge for us to change our perspective on worship. What a blessing that we can lift our thanksgiving to God without persecution. How wonderful we don't have to thank Him through a saint or priest. So be demonstrative with your gratitude, giving God the glory and praise with passion every day.

....

....

....

....

....

....

....

....

*God, it's my honor and privilege to praise Your holy name,
and let my heart feel delighted when I do. In Jesus' name. Amen.*

Meditating on God's Goodness

For Yahweh is always good and ready to receive you. He's so loving that it will amaze you—so kind that it will astound you! And he is famous for his faithfulness toward all. Everyone knows our God can be trusted, for he keeps his promises to every generation!

PSALM 100:5 TPT

Spend today meditating on God's goodness! Chances are we don't do this on the regular because life comes at us fast, and we're focused on just staying afloat. But choosing to acknowledge the awesomeness and magnificence of God helps keep our hearts grounded in faith for whatever comes our way. So be comforted in knowing He is *always good* and *always ready* when we need Him.

Think of the ways God's love has amazed you. How have you seen Him be kind in your circumstances? Remember the times He was faithful to follow through. Meditate on the moments God's trustworthiness floored you. Today, be filled with joy as your mind focuses on what an awe-inspiring God you serve.

....

....

....

....

....

....

....

....

God, my heart is full of memories about Your goodness. Thank You for being a loving Father. In Jesus' name. Amen.

Let God's Words Lead

By your words I can see where I'm going; they throw a beam
of light on my dark path. I've committed myself and I'll
never turn back from living by your righteous order.
PSALM 119:105–106 MSG

When we follow God's leading, it blesses our lives. How? Because it becomes the lens we view life through. And that gives us perspective, so we can navigate from a place of strength rather than a place of weakness. It provides clarity above chaos, enabling us to make wise choices. As we heed God's words, they keep us walking in the direction He's planned all along.

Ask God for the ability to see life through His eyes. When the challenges you're facing begin to blur and fog your understanding, let that be a red flag to take it right to God. He will graciously illuminate the dark path so you can walk out each day in His will.

....
....
....
....
....
....
....
....
....

God, Your words bring life and understanding to my heart and light my way, even in the darkest times. Thank You for this gift. Let it guide and encourage me always! In Jesus' name. Amen.

Putting You Back Together Again

Everything's falling apart on me, GOD; put me together again with your Word. Adorn me with your finest sayings, GOD; teach me your holy rules. My life is as close as my own hands, but I don't forget what you have revealed.
PSALM 119:107–109 MSG

Take heart, friend! When you have days where it feels like everything is falling apart, God promises to put you back together. Through His Word, you'll find the comfort you're craving. And you'll find hope throughout its pages as you read reminders of His restoration. Everything we need to live in freedom and victory is found through God, and His Word is where we learn what He's capable of and willing to do.

Where do you need rebuilding in your life today? Have you lost credibility with someone important to you? Have you not followed through on promises? Are you walking out the natural consequences of your sin or someone else's? Start each day steeped in God's Word, letting it put you back together again.

....

....

....

....

....

....

....

God, every time I open Your Word, let it be the glue that restores the broken pieces of my life. In Jesus' name. Amen.

Soul-Vibrating Joy and Hope

I am filled with joy and my soul vibrates with exuberant hope, because of the Eternal my God; for He has dressed me with the garment of salvation, wrapped me with the robe of righteousness. It's as though I'm dressed for my wedding day, in the very best: a bridegroom's garland and a bride's jewels.
ISAIAH 61:10 VOICE

Want to have an amazing day? Even in the middle of the difficult struggles you're facing right now, it's possible to be filled with soul-vibrating joy and hope. It's a supernatural blessing that's often misunderstood by others. They look at your life and feel exhausted. They see no easy answers or viable way out. So, when you are standing strong, they are confused.

Tell anyone who asks about your positive attitude in the middle of negative circumstances that it's all because of God. You are loved. You have been made righteous. Your eternal salvation is secured. And those wonderful truths trump any earthly worry any day.

....

....

....

....

....

....

....

....

....

God, I love that You are a mystery and Your ways are unexplainable.
Thank You for all that faith affords me. In Jesus' name. Amen.

In Awe of God's Splendor

God's splendor is a tale that is told, written in the stars. Space itself speaks his story through the marvels of the heavens. His truth is on tour in the starry vault of the sky, showing his skill in creation's craftsmanship.
PSALM 19:1 TPT

Every day is a new opportunity to sit in awe of God's splendor. Have you ever stared at the mountains in wonderment? Have you taken in the vastness of an ocean and responded with astonishment? What about staring into the night sky? One can't help but marvel at the intricacies of the stars and planets.

Today, choose to slow down. Rather than rush from one thing to the next, ask God for your eyes and ears to notice His creative craftsmanship daily. Give yourself time to take it all in. Allow yourself to be amazed and surprised by the Lord's attention to detail. And let yourself be deeply moved as you celebrate the world He has made.

....
....
....
....
....
....
....
....
....

God, open my heart so I feel complete reverence as I go through my day and notice Your fingerprints all over the world. Let's rejoice in Your handiwork together! In Jesus' name. Amen.

Cleansed from Secret and Selfish Sins

Keep cleansing me, God, and keep me from my secret,
selfish sins; may they never rule over me! For only then will
I be free from fault and remain innocent of rebellion.
PSALM 19:13 TPT

Secret sin has a way of ruining even the best of days. In our rebellion, we believe that what we're doing out of the public eye remains hidden. But the truth is, God sees it. Nothing is blocked from His view. And He understands the complexity of why those things rule over you. God has a full picture, while we do not.

Let God be your closest companion. Don't shy away from being honest, because He knows it all. Remember, there's no condemnation in Christ. You can trust that God's love is safe and secure. So let Him untangle you from any secret and selfish sin. Invite the Lord into the deepest parts of your life, and watch how His love heals and restores the broken places.

....

....

....

....

....

....

....

God, I confess my sins and rebellion to You right now.
Cleanse me and renew me daily. Let my love for You be what
drives me to live a righteous life. In Jesus' name. Amen.

Acceptable and Pleasing

So may the words of my mouth, my meditation-thoughts, and every movement of my heart be always pure and pleasing, acceptable before your eyes, Yahweh, my only Redeemer, my Protector.
PSALM 19:14 TPT

This is a weighty pursuit, amen? Of course, we want our words to be acceptable to God. We want our thoughts to glorify only Him. And we hope that our hearts are filled with pure motives every day. But the truth is, this is a bear to walk out—at least on our own.

Start each morning in prayer, asking the Lord to make this pursuit possible. Tell Him where you feel weak and where you need His help. Let God know where you're falling short in your faith walk. Be assured that when you ask for help to walk out a righteous life, He will make it so. When you lean on Him, God will enable you to live in a way that's acceptable and pleasing. And each day, you will find reasons to be full of joy and peace.

....

....

....

....

....

....

....

....

God, give me everything I need to make my words and actions bring You glory! I love You. In Jesus' name. Amen.

Everything You Need

Strengthen them with Your infinite power, according to Your glorious might, so that they will have everything they need to hold on and endure hardship patiently and joyfully.

<small>COLOSSIANS 1:11 VOICE</small>

In today's verse, Paul is praying this for the church. He knows, without question, that God must be the one to make this prayer a reality. The strength of the church will be a God-given blessing, and He will equip them with what they need to walk difficult roads. And with His help, they'll be able to persevere through tough times and endure with a joyful attitude.

Let this prayer from Paul cover you today too. Read it again with your circumstances in view. How does it encourage you? How does this prayer give you endurance for the journey? How does it settle your anxious heart? Friend, let your only hope be anchored in God. He sees you; He loves you; and He will strengthen you for the next step.

....

....

....

....

....

....

....

....

God, my life is only good because You are in it. Every day, You're the one who promises to meet every need. . . and You do! My heart is full. In Jesus' name. Amen.

Discovering God's Word

When I discovered Your words, I ate them up: they were my great
joy and my heart's delight. I am Yours, and I bear the name
of the Eternal God, Commander of heavenly armies.
JEREMIAH 15:16 VOICE

Can you remember a time when you read a scripture that seemed to leap off the page? It fell fresh on your heart, even though you may have read it before. Sometimes the sweetest thing is to rediscover God's Word. It is alive and active; and when we invest time in its pages, we will be blessed.

When your heart feels delighted by scripture, don't waste that moment. Meditate on those key verses all day. Chew on it with the Lord, asking Him to speak deeper into your soul. Share it with friends. And from a place of reverent gratitude, thank God for highlighting it at just the right moment.

....

....

....

....

....

....

....

....

God, I love that Your Word is relevant in my life today and full of
wonderment. Fill me with a desire to spend time sitting in
scripture and discovering what You want to say to me.
I'm interested and listening! In Jesus' name. Amen.

Delighted by Weakness

So I'm not defeated by my weakness, but delighted! For when I feel my weakness and endure mistreatment—when I'm surrounded with troubles on every side and face persecution because of my love for Christ—I am made yet stronger. For my weakness becomes a portal to God's power.
2 CORINTHIANS 12:10 TPT

What a powerful truth: our weakness is "a portal to God's power." It's so counterintuitive from what the world preaches. From a young age, we're encouraged to be strong and independent. We are taught to be self-made and proud of it. And often, the last thing we want anyone to know is that we feel exhausted, fragile, and vulnerable.

But God sees things differently. Accurately. And when we feel inadequate, He's there to make up the difference. Where we fall short, God fills in the gaps. Our weakness isn't negative. Instead, it's expected because of our human condition. Daily, be quick to tell God where you need His power, and be delighted that it can flow through you.

....

....

....

....

....

....

....

....

God, help me not feel defeated by my weakness but grateful for Your strength in me. In Jesus' name. Amen.

The Depth of His Compassion

Look on me with a heart of mercy, O God, according to Your generous love. According to Your great compassion, wipe out every consequence of my shameful crimes. Thoroughly wash me, inside and out, of all my crooked deeds. Cleanse me from my sins.
PSALM 51:1–2 VOICE

One of the most beautiful things about God is the depth of His compassion for those who love Him. It's a powerful force that blesses the heart of a believer because it assures that we're free from condemnation. We may have to walk out the natural consequences of our sin, but the Lord will not heap guilt and shame on us. He won't dismiss us or turn His back in disgust. Scripture says God's love is generous and His heart is full of mercy, and that releases us from any expectations of perfection.

Don't let the weight of sin keep you from enjoying every day to its fullest! There's no good reason for it. Instead, confess your wrongdoing and then ask God to reveal His peace.

....

....

....

....

....

....

....

God, thank You for the gift of love and compassion. In Jesus' name. Amen.

God Knows What He's Doing

"I know what I'm doing. I have it all planned out—plans to take care of you, not abandon you, plans to give you the future you hope for."
JEREMIAH 29:11 MSG

What a relief to know that when you don't have any idea what comes next, God has it all planned out. You don't have to go into your day with answers, because God already has them. When life gets wonky and you feel destabilized, you don't have to partner with fear. And every time those feelings of hopelessness surface, you can trust the Lord with your unknown future.

Friend, God has plans to take care of you. He's in it for the long haul because you're worth His time and energy. You're His beloved creation, but God didn't stop there. He didn't just make you. In addition, He made plans for your future—plans to delight you. God decided to be with you always. And every day, you can trust He's involved from morning till night.

....

....

....

....

....

....

....

....

....

....

God, I believe You have my best at heart always. I know Your plans are for my good and Your glory. In Jesus' name. Amen.

Seeking God in Earnest

"When you call on me, when you come and pray to me, I'll listen.
When you come looking for me, you'll find me. Yes, when you get
serious about finding me and want it more than anything else,
I'll make sure you won't be disappointed." GOD's Decree.

JEREMIAH 29:12–14 MSG

Let the truth of these verses bless you. They are packed with affirmation and encouragement to pursue God with fervor and ask for His help in troubling times. They encourage persistent prayer and pure motives. And they challenge you to prioritize God above all else in your life.

Take your relationship with God seriously. If you are dabbling, straddling the fence of faith, it's time to make a declaration of belief and a decision of salvation. The Lord is waiting and ready for your devotion. He promises it won't end in disappointment. Choose daily to seek God with all your heart and be blessed!

God, help me seek You in earnest every day. From now on, I am
going to get serious about growing and nurturing my relationship
with You. I love You, Father! In Jesus' name. Amen.

Miracles Still Happen

We laughed and laughed and overflowed with gladness. We were left shouting for joy and singing your praise. All the nations saw it and joined in, saying, "The Lord has done great miracles for them!" Yes, he did mighty miracles and we are overjoyed!
PSALM 126:2–3 TPT

There are some who believe God no longer performs miracles, but that's simply not true. The miracle may be the restoration of a marriage on divorce's doorstep. It may be a prodigal child who has returned. It may be a disease that disappears without treatment. It could even be a miraculous financial windfall that covers bills down to the penny.

Ask the Lord to give you the spiritual eyes to see His hand moving in your life, because it is moving, whether you see it or not. And when you become aware of His goodness, let your heart overflow with gladness. Shout for joy and sing His praises to anyone who will listen. These are faith-building moments that help change lives.

....
....
....
....
....
....
....
....

God, I give You the credit and the glory for every good thing in my life. I know they all come from You. In Jesus' name. Amen.

When You're Scared to Open Up to God

Open up before GOD, keep nothing back; he'll do whatever
needs to be done: He'll validate your life in the clear light of
day and stamp you with approval at high noon.
PSALM 37:5–6 MSG

To say it's challenging to be authentic and honest may be an epic understatement. Chances are even our besties don't know the deepest, darkest parts of our souls. Few understand the things that hurt the most and make us feel unloved. But it's risky to open up to anyone, because once we do, the truth is out there. Sometimes it just feels scary to expose ourselves like that.

It might be difficult to set our feelings aside and let God in. But as a believer, your job is to choose to trust Him. Scripture is full of reminders that He is faithful and trustworthy. So make it a daily practice to open your heart to Him and share what burdens it. In return, you will receive peace and comfort and validation.

God, give me courage to take a leap of faith and trust You with my
heart. I need Your help to get started. In Jesus' name. Amen.

Beware of Self-Interest

*Quiet down before God, be prayerful before him. Don't bother with
those who climb the ladder, who elbow their way to the top.*
PSALM 37:7 MSG

As believers, we should not try to make it to celebrity status. Our goal shouldn't
be to work our way to the top. Too often, when it is, we're working in our own
self-interest, and we hurt people along the way. We end up stepping on them in
our pursuit of prominence. If God wants us elevated to a position of leadership,
we can fully trust that He will do it at the right time in the right way.

Instead, what if we walked through each day prayerfully? Not only would
that make for the best days ever, but it would also keep us in close communica-
tion with God. It would help our hearts stay in the right place, showing respect
and care for others as we honor Him. And it would allow us to discern if any
promotion or elevation that presents itself is from God or man.

*God, remind me this world is not my home. I want to store
up my treasures in heaven. In Jesus' name. Amen.*

Working for the Good

Turn your back on evil, work for the good and don't quit. GOD loves this kind of thing, never turns away from his friends. Live this way and you've got it made, but bad eggs will be tossed out.
PSALM 37:27–28 MSG

You are to be light and salt to the world. Your words and actions should be what points others to God in heaven. And, when the opportunity presents itself, you should authentically share your testimony of how God has shown up in your circumstances. That is how you work for good as suggested in today's passage of scripture.

This isn't a call for perfection. We all know that's not what God expects, nor is it what's attainable. Instead, this is a challenge to live with purpose and passion, full of faith every day. When we are willing to walk the path of righteousness—even if a little shaky at times—our choices will bless God and encourage others.

....

....

....

....

....

....

....

....

God, bless me with the courage and confidence to work for the good each day and in all circumstances. I want my life to bless and delight You. In Jesus' name. Amen.

A Spacious and Free Life

The spacious, free life is from God, it's also protected and safe.
God-strengthened, we're delivered from evil—when we run to him, he saves us.
PSALM 37:39–40 MSG

What do you think it means to have a spacious life? Maybe it means we're not bogged down by a to-do list or our calendars. Maybe it means we don't have daily difficulties pressing on us from every side. Or maybe it means that, regardless of what life brings, we're able to find margin because God protects and saves those who love Him.

Having a free and spacious life paints a beautiful picture, doesn't it? Well, this is the kind of life that's available to every believer. We are God-strengthened for the battles that lie ahead—the ones that can't crush or crowd us. So, decide today that when you feel the pressure mounting, you'll run right to God. Even in the middle of your day, fall into the arms of the Father who will protect and save you every time.

....

....

....

....

....

....

....

God, I want a free and spacious life. Thank You for making it available
to me through Your generous love. In Jesus' name. Amen.

Joy in Following God's Way

I find more joy in following what you tell me to do than in chasing after all the wealth of the world. I set my heart on your precepts and pay close attention to all your ways.

PSALM 119:14–15 TPT

Yes! This is called righteous living, which simply means living in a right relationship with God. It's choosing to see the world through the lens of faith. It's following God over the world's persuasions. It's setting aside your fleshly desires and doing what you know glorifies the Lord. It's starting your day in prayer, asking God for the confidence and courage to make hard choices. And when you are intentional to live this way, it will become a source of joy. Knowing you're delighting God will fuel your faith.

Let every day bring you another step closer to Him. Ask for an infusion of His power and wisdom and discernment so you're able to follow God with fervor. There are great blessings in store when you live your life to please Him.

....

....

....

....

....

....

....

....

....

God, I choose Your way over anything the world has to offer me. In Jesus' name. Amen.

It Comes from God

Your displeasure rests with those who are arrogant, who think they know everything; you rebuke the rebellious who refuse your laws.
PSALM 119:21 TPT

Every day is a choice to be humble. We must remember that our lives should point others to God and nothing else. Any stroke of brilliance is from Him. Our creativity was baked in when we were formed. We may have worked hard for a degree, but God planned our steps and equipped us with the tools to do so. Our success is His provision. Our talents are His gift. And our desire to do good is His plan. We may have done the work, but God gets the glory.

Be ready and willing to acknowledge God rather than pat yourself on the back. Thank Him for giving you the skill set, the courage, the revelation, the work ethic, and the perseverance. And thank Him for giving you faith to follow His will and ways for your life.

God, keep me from being arrogant—it's ugly and ungodly. I know all good things come from You alone! In Jesus' name. Amen.

Fading Away

Lord, I'm fading away. I'm discouraged and lying in the dust;
revive me by your word, just like you promised you would.
I've poured out my life before you, and you've always been there
for me. So now I ask: teach me more of your holy decrees.
PSALM 119:25–26 TPT

Have you ever felt as if you're "fading away"? Those are very descriptive words! Maybe you've had a rough season that's left you discouraged. Maybe you don't feel seen by others—like you've lost importance in their life. Do you feel lonely or cast aside? Maybe you're divorced or grieving the death of a husband. Maybe you're single and an empty-nester or you feel alone in marriage. Regardless, it's left you disheartened and hopeless.

Every day that you feel this way, open God's Word. It has the power to reverse the *fading away* feeling so prevalent in your life. As a matter of fact, scripture will enable you to have a beautiful day as you commune with God. He will speak value and worth into your heart. And He will always be there to pick you up.

....

....

....

....

....

....

....

....

God, thank You for seeing me. In Jesus' name. Amen.

Don't Be a Mess-Maker

Lord, don't allow me to make a mess of my life, for I cling to
your commands and follow them as closely as I can.
PSALM 119:31 TPT

The psalmist is desperate for God's intervention. He obviously understood the human condition and how we often make a mess of our lives. Think back to a situation where you could relate. Chances are it wasn't your desire, but even our best-laid plans fail from time to time. Amen? So how wonderful to know that we can ask God to help us be blessings-bringers and not mess-makers.

How can we do this? By living out God's commands. And it's through time in His Word that we learn what these directives are. The Bible teaches us how to love and forgive. It teaches us how to live with passion and purpose. It unpacks compassion. It shows us how to create healthy boundaries. And it reveals important ways we can make a difference in the lives of others every single day—turning good days into *great* days!

....

....

....

....

....

....

....

....

God, empower me through Your commands to live a
life that glorifies You! In Jesus' name. Amen.

When We Feel Persecuted

Defend me from the criticism I face for keeping your beautiful words.
PSALM 119:39 TPT

It can be very difficult to be a believer in today's world. Just as the Bible says, there will come a time when we are persecuted for being Christ followers. It will be challenging to stand up for the truth. And we will need God's strength and comfort to help us navigate those difficult times. Friend, don't ever hesitate to ask Him for help.

Even when we face criticism from the world for honoring God with our choices, it doesn't have to rob us of the joy each day can bring. It's a matter of perspective. Our spirits can be soaring because of the connection we have with God, even if our bodies and minds are lagging a bit. We can stand strong with a victory mindset—keeping our eyes on the bigger picture—and trusting God to be our defender and restorer.

....

....

....

....

....

....

....

....

....

God, don't let me cower when criticism comes my way.
Instead, let me activate my faith and find my resolve to
stand firm as a believer. In Jesus' name. Amen.

Complete Freedom

I will walk with you in complete freedom, for I seek to follow your every command.
PSALM 119:45 TPT

How different would your day look if you chose to walk with God in complete freedom? Would it free you up from performance-based relationships? Would it prevent you from gauging your worth by the world's standards? Would it allow you to worship in your own way without worrying about criticism? Would it give you confidence to show care and compassion to the "least of these"?

Jesus stepped out of heaven, died on the cross, and rose three days later to give you complete freedom. This gift is yours for the taking if you accept Jesus as your Savior. And when you live any way other than in complete freedom, you are robbing yourself of His perfect gift. Before your feet hit the floor in the morning, ask God to give you the courage to embrace your God-given freedom in every way throughout your day.

....

....

....

....

....

....

....

....

God, thank You for the gift of complete freedom through Your Son. Help me make the choice to embrace that freedom with resolve and walk it out daily. In Jesus' name. Amen.

The Promises of God

Lord, never forget the promises you've made to me, for they
are my hope and confidence. In all of my affliction I find great
comfort in your promises, for they have kept me alive!
PSALM 119:49–50 TPT

When God makes a promise, it's a promise kept. He is simply unable to go against His word. And you can find His promises all throughout the Bible. From the books of Genesis to Revelation, He is decisive and clear. You will see again and again how God did what He said He would do. Even more, we can be assured those promises are still applicable today.

Here's where it's tricky and we get confused. We have human expectations for how our divine God will fulfill the promises set forth. We ask with our desired response from Him in mind, forgetting our ways are not His ways. Our thoughts are not His thoughts. So choosing to stand in hope and confidence will result in peace and comfort.

....

....

....

....

....

....

....

....

God, help me trust that You will fulfill Your promises in the
right way and at the right time. Your promises bless me,
and I will in turn glorify You. In Jesus' name. Amen.

Changing Our Line of Thinking

Throughout the night I think of you, dear God; I treasure your every word to me. All this joy is mine as I follow your ways!
PSALM 119:55–56 TPT

So many of us have sleepless nights because we're stressed and worried. It's often in the quiet of night that our minds get the best of us. It's where we imagine horrible outcomes and endings. As we lay in the dark, we replay the day's events, analyzing the situation ad nauseum. And it makes for a terrible tomorrow.

But what if we followed the example of the psalmist in today's scripture? What if we changed our line of thinking from anxious thoughts to God thoughts? It would be an intentional choice to shift our hearts from all that could go wrong to the awesomeness of God. We'd focus on His goodness instead of our messiness. His promises rather than our problems. And it would make for a terrific tomorrow!

....

....

....

....

....

....

....

....

God, let any late-night frustrations drive me to activate my faith so I can focus my thoughts on You instead of me. In Jesus' name. Amen.

When You Need God's Comfort

Send your kind mercy-kiss to comfort me, your servant, just like you promised you would. Love me tenderly so I can go on, for I delight in your life-giving truth.
PSALM 119:76–77 TPT

There are moments when the only way we'll find comfort is in the hands of God. No thing or person will do. The pain is too deep. The grief is too overwhelming. The fear is too overpowering. The worry is too crushing. And our souls know it's only in His arms that we'll find the peace and rest we're desperately craving.

As you go through your day, tell God your need for comfort. Remind Him of the promises He's whispered to you or the ones you've read in His Word—not because God needs the reminder but because *you* do. You need a dose of hope that sticks. You need to be surrounded by His truth. It's often in these moments that we need to remember God loves us and is for us.

....

....

....

....

....

....

....

....

God, I need the kindness and comfort only You can bring. Surround me with Your tender love so I feel safe and secure. In Jesus' name. Amen.

Taking the Pressure Off

I've learned that there is nothing perfect in this imperfect world except
your words, for they bring such fantastic freedom into my life!
PSALM 119:96 TPT

Choose to boldly live by these words every day. And friend, get off the perfection treadmill that makes you strive to meet the world's standards. Think about how it would calm your anxious heart to know—*to truly believe*—there's nothing perfect in this imperfect world. Even on your best day, you'll fall short of some expectation somewhere.

There's a beautiful freedom that comes from accepting this world—and the people in it—as flawed and faulty. Honestly, it takes the pressure off! We don't have to fit the mold or be accepted by the "in" crowd. Truly, it's okay to let your faith show, because living by godly guidelines is good in God's eyes. And the only perfect thing in this world is His Word, which is alive and active every day.

God, help me to stop pressuring myself to be perfect for the
world. The world's expectations are not my standard of
measurement! Instead, let me find acceptance and love
through Your Word. In Jesus' name. Amen.

Do Your Morals Bend?

I refused to bend my morals when temptation was before me so that I could become obedient to your Word. I refuse to turn away from difficult truths, for you yourself have taught me to love your words.
PSALM 119:101–102 TPT

Chances are you face opportunities to bend your morals every day. Between breakfast and dinner, there are countless temptations that sashay through your life. From telling little white lies to participating in catastrophic moral failures, it's because of God's Word you're able to stay strong.

Every choice you make to be obedient to the Lord will be rewarded. This is a powerful concept shared all throughout the Bible, and it's still true today. The world praises flexibility, but the moral truths in God's Word do not bend. And that is great news, because it's not a moving target. You know exactly how to make it a good day that pleases the Lord.

....

....

....

....

....

....

....

....

....

God, my heart's desire is to obey Your Word. Give me courage to obey, even when it's hard. Give me confidence to stand up for what is right, even when it's unpopular. In Jesus' name. Amen.

Bruised and Broken

I'm bruised and broken, overwhelmed by it all;
breathe life into me again by your living word.
PSALM 119:107 TPT

Friend, what has you bruised and broken today? What's causing you to feel overwhelmed? Is the prescribed treatment not working? Has your husband threatened to leave the marriage? Were you fired from a job you dearly loved? Have you lost someone and the grief feels too big? Are you moving to a new city, far away from friends and family? Was your secret sin exposed? Are you out of answers?

Take your bruised and broken heart right to God, letting Him breathe His restorative breath into your weary soul. Sit in scripture and watch as He brings encouragement through the Word. You may be nursing wounds from the world, but you can experience God's joy and peace at the same time. It doesn't negate your pain; it just allows you to see the bigger picture of what the Lord is doing in your day.

....

....

....

....

....

....

....

....

God, use Your Word to breathe life into me again. I need Your
divine perspective so I can stand in victory. In Jesus' name. Amen.

Wrapped in God's Word

You're my place of quiet retreat, and your wraparound presence
becomes my shield as I wrap myself in your Word!
PSALM 119:114 TPT

The Word of God is supernatural. In its pages, you will find a prescription for what ails you. You'll find encouragement to take the next step. It's full of wisdom and discernment to help guide you through the mountaintops and valleys. You will learn how to have self-control. You'll see examples of God's faithfulness and be inspired by stories that demonstrate His unwavering trustworthiness. There will be scriptures to challenge you and others that bring conviction. And it's where God reveals Himself to those who love Him.

Every day, wrap the Word of God around you. Let it be what affirms your faith and gives you a positive outlook. If you'll allow it, the Lord will fill your love bucket with His Word. Even more, when you let His Word be your place of quiet retreat, it will heal the broken places and restore your energy. The Bible is the best day-maker!

....

....

....

....

....

....

....

....

God, Your Word is a gift to me, and I will treasure
it every day. In Jesus' name. Amen.

Be a Bold Lover of Jesus

Lord, strengthen my inner being by the promises of your Word
so that I may live faithful and unashamed for you.
PSALM 119:116 TPT

What a blessing for us that God included this verse in His Word. This is an honest plea that comes from a real and raw place in the psalmist's heart. This is a cry for help, an appeal for an infusion of God's strength. There's no doubt this writer is a bold lover of God. What a pleasing request for His holy ears.

It's challenging to be intrepid in a world less inclined to accept Jesus. Sometimes that reality causes us to keep our faith tucked away so we avoid questions or ridicule. We profess powerful love for the Lord—just not in public. But that's not how God intended us to live. Friend, you have the freedom to have joy in Jesus! Start your morning in the Bible, and watch it embolden your day.

God, strengthen me from the inside out so I can live
faithful and unashamed to glorify Your name without
the fear of man. In Jesus' name. Amen.

They Can Coexist

Even though my troubles overwhelm me with anguish, I still delight and cherish every message you speak to me. Give me more revelation so that I can live for you, for nothing is more pure and eternal than your truth.
PSALM 119:143–144 TPT

Did you catch that? It's possible to have joy in the Lord even when you feel overwhelmed by life. You can be in the battle of your life and still have good days! Your struggle in the natural doesn't have to interfere with the condition of your heart in the spiritual. But so often we decide the two can't coexist. We lose hope, and our faith falters. And before we're aware, this becomes the beginning of a victim mentality. It's how we justify living offended. It kills our zest for life.

But, friend, God is bigger than any problem you're facing today. Let Him give you fresh revelation of His goodness. Ask for a deeper understanding of the truth and a robust joy for His Word. Choose joy over the junk that's bringing you down.

God, keep my eyes focused on You over everything else! In Jesus' name. Amen.

God Is on Your Side

Take my side and defend me in these sufferings; redeem me
and revive me, just like you promised you would.
PSALM 119:154 TPT

We all want people on our side when things go south. We believe there's safety in numbers, so we go about recruiting a team who will support and validate us. We want others to defend our name or our ideas or our interests, especially when we feel we've been wronged. But we don't need worldly help. We need divine intervention. God is the only one you need on your team.

He is ready to redeem and revive you when you ask. It's a promise—a guarantee for those who love Him. He is just and kind and will bring righteousness into your circumstances. So don't hesitate to share the details of your heartache with God. Ask Him to defend you, making right what has gone wrong. And then leave it in His hands as you find joy and happiness in your day.

....
....
....
....
....
....
....
....
....
....

God, what a relief to know You are on my side. Even more,
You're the only one I need! In Jesus' name. Amen.

God Is Arranging Everything

We are confident that God is able to orchestrate everything to work toward something good and beautiful when we love Him and accept His invitation to live according to His plan.

ROMANS 8:28 VOICE

No matter what you're facing today, have faith that God's hands are working in it. He's always in the details. And what may look insurmountable through our eyes doesn't intimidate our Father in heaven one bit. As a matter of fact, He has a supernatural way of choreographing the joys and challenges in our lives and creating something good. Even the best multitasker couldn't keep up.

Here's why that kind of news can brighten our day: it allows us to stay hopeful that our current struggles won't do us in. We can trust that God will redeem our heartaches and make sense of them. As believers, we have a front row seat to watch Him work miracles in our mess. So, live with joy, knowing God is arranging good and beautiful things every day.

God, help my heart rest in the truth that You're orchestrating everything in my life to work toward something good and beautiful. In Jesus' name. Amen.

The Spirit Articulates Your Prayers

A similar thing happens when we pray. We are weak and do not know how to pray, so the Spirit steps in and articulates prayers for us with groaning too profound for words.
ROMANS 8:26 VOICE

Don't get tangled up in the idea that your prayers must be perfect. You may not always have the most eloquent words to share. Sometimes your prayers may consist of a guttural cry from deep within. Maybe all you can manage to say is the name of Jesus over and over again. Because the Spirit is in the hearts of the believers, we have an advocate to articulate our imperfect prayers to the Father. The Spirit knows exactly what we're trying to say—every detail of what's marinating in our hearts.

When your heart is burdened, pray. Don't let any insecurities or a loss of words stop you. And don't try to be someone you're not when you're talking to God, looking for big words and melodic phrases. Instead, rejoice in knowing the Holy Spirit will always fill in the gaps.

....

....

....

....

....

....

....

God, thank You for the gift of Your Holy Spirit in my life! In Jesus' name. Amen.

Fear Nothing

So what should we say about all of this? If God is on our side, then tell me: whom should we fear? If He did not spare His own Son, but handed Him over on our account, then don't you think that He will graciously give us all things with Him?
ROMANS 8:31–32 VOICE

Starting today, let there be a little spring in your step. Let a big, beaming smile be all over your face. Let your eyes twinkle with delight. Because, friend, if God is on your side, you have *nothing* to fear.

Chances are you've heard that a million times, but let it sink in right now. First, if you're a believer, then God has your back. That in and of itself is worthy of a celebration! But it's because He's intimately involved with you that fear has no power in your life. When you get the phone call, when the bank overdrafts, when the relationship ends, and when the diagnosis comes, remember that God is on your side. He will work everything out. And you're going to be okay.

God, I shall fear nothing because of You! In Jesus' name. Amen.

No, Nothing

For I have every confidence that nothing—not death, life, heavenly
messengers, dark spirits, the present, the future, spiritual powers,
height, depth, nor any created thing—can come between us and
the love of God revealed in the Anointed, Jesus our Lord.
ROMANS 8:38–39 VOICE

Even when our plan is to love someone forever, things often get in the way that make it impossible. The flip side is also true. We expect to be loved unconditionally, and our hearts are broken when it doesn't happen. Each one of us has experienced this kind of pain and carries the scars to prove it.

So, when we read scripture that promises nothing will interrupt God's love, it can be hard to believe. We're conditioned for performance-based relationships. We've experienced rejection and abandonment from those we trusted. If this resonates, ask God to make the truth of His unbreakable love real to you. Ask for a deeper level of trust. And then let it be the undercurrent that makes your days overflow with confidence.

....

....

....

....

....

....

....

....

God, thank You that nothing can separate us. Bring
that beautiful promise of full acceptance to full bloom
in my heart. In Jesus' name. Amen.

Asking for Divine Discernment

My dear friends, don't believe everything you hear. Carefully weigh and examine what people tell you. Not everyone who talks about God comes from God. There are a lot of lying preachers loose in the world.

1 JOHN 4:1 MSG

Let discernment be a daily request of God. Without it, we simply won't have the ability to discern every right from every wrong. We won't know when to follow someone's suggestions or turn from them and run. And we will fall prey to the wrong teaching of God's Word. We'll end up relying on the interpretation of another person instead of asking the Lord for revelation. Friend, divine discernment keeps us from blindly following false teachers and lying preachers.

The goal of each day should be to grow closer to God. As believers, we should live with the kind of joy the world can't match. Our words and actions should highlight our love for God and point to Him in heaven. And having discernment helps bring these to fruition, giving us glorious and fruitful days in relationship with Him.

....
....
....
....
....
....
....

God, help me discern who and what glorifies You and who and what does not. In Jesus' name. Amen.

No Room for Fear

*There is no room in love for fear. Well-formed love banishes
fear. Since fear is crippling, a fearful life—fear of death,
fear of judgment—is one not yet fully formed in love.*
1 JOHN 4:18 MSG

When your heart is filled with the truth of God's love for you, it produces a
boldness. Fear loses its grip because you know He will show up. You try new
things. You stand up for injustices and speak out, advocating for righteous
living. Because of faith, you're confident God is working all things together
for your good, giving you courage to follow the path He's set before you. And,
friend, it looks good on you.

Living in fear will do nothing but ruin your day. It makes you ineffective for
the kingdom. It makes you doubt God's sovereignty and goodness. It keeps you
stuck and unable to fulfill the calling on your life. Fear is *not* for the believer.
Let God reveal the depth of His love, and live with passion and purpose!

*God, there is no room for fear in my life because I am
fully loved by You! In Jesus' name. Amen.*

The Challenge to Love Others

The command we have from Christ is blunt: Loving God
includes loving people. You've got to love both.
1 JOHN 4:21 MSG

Have you ever thought it easy to love God but not His people? The truth is, humanity is tricky because we are imperfect people, living in an imperfect world, trying to navigate the ups and downs of our imperfect relationships. While we don't always understand God's will or His ways, it's often easier to turn our heart toward God because of our faith. His people, however, are a different story. They are often the reasons we feel unloved, insecure, and inadequate. And so, in self-preservation, we close ourselves off to community.

But we can't love God and not His people. They go together. Anyone who claims differently is simply wrong. When we truly understand this, it will provide a new perspective to live by each day. We'll learn to see others through God's eyes often because we've asked for it through prayer. Our hearts will become compassionate and caring for all because we've chosen to accept the package deal.

God, give me a desire to love everyone just as
You command. In Jesus' name. Amen.

Here to Broadcast

But you are God's chosen treasure—priests who are kings, a spiritual "nation" set apart as God's devoted ones. He called you out of darkness to experience his marvelous light, and now he claims you as his very own. He did this so that you would broadcast his glorious wonders throughout the world.

1 Peter 2:9 tpt

Today's verse is important and should be on the tip of the tongue of every believer. It not only solidifies our identity but also reveals our calling. It affirms who we are and why we're breathing air on planet earth. Every time you doubt you're here on purpose and for a purpose, revisit this scripture. It will settle your anxious heart as it bolsters your confidence.

The bottom line is that God gave you standing so you could show others His wonders. Through your healing and restoration, the Lord's plan is for the sharing of your testimony to those who will listen. God wants your life circumstances to broadcast His goodness. He chose you to live each day to its fullest, encouraging others to embrace faith.

....

....

....

....

....

....

....

....

....

God, use me and my life. I am Yours! In Jesus' name. Amen.

Never Alone

Take a decisive stand against him and resist his every attack with strong, vigorous faith. For you know that your believing brothers and sisters around the world are experiencing the same kinds of troubles you endure.

1 PETER 5:9 TPT

So often we feel alone in the battle. It's an isolating experience because we assume others can't fully understand what we're going through. They can bring us meals, sit with us in court, help navigate the doctor's appointments, and pray with fervor. But we still end up feeling alone.

What changes that mindset is the awesome truth there are other believers around the world experiencing the *same* things. They're facing the *same* troubles you are. What you're struggling with, they are struggling with too. So don't walk around thinking your situation is unique, because it's not. And friend, that is a blessing! You are not alone. Let that strengthen your resolve to stand strong against every evil force, because you are linking arms with others doing the same.

....

....

....

....

....

....

....

....

God, what a gift to know I am not alone. Thank You for the reminder that we're in this together. In Jesus' name. Amen

The Blessing of Briefness

And then, after your brief suffering, the God of all loving grace,
who has called you to share in his eternal glory in Christ,
will personally and powerfully restore you and make you stronger
than ever. Yes, he will set you firmly in place and build you up.

1 PETER 5:10 TPT

What a beautiful benefit of being a believer! We know suffering is a part of the human experience. We've been told throughout scripture our expectation should include difficulties and challenges. We know life is hard, brings pain, and isn't fair. But what we sometimes forget is the blessing of briefness.

God's Word is clear that our suffering will be short-lived. It's transitory. Our struggles won't last forever. And on the other side, we will be restored and made stronger. That means there's purpose in the pain we must endure on earth. We don't have to mope around, joyless and sad, because we know this momentary messiness will yield a magnificent message of God's loving grace in the end.

....

....

....

....

....

....

....

....

God, thank You for the blessing of briefness and the
gift of restoration. In Jesus' name. Amen.

Giving It to God

Pour out all your worries and stress upon him and leave them there, for he always tenderly cares for you.
1 PETER 5:7 TPT

When you lighten your emotional load, it frees you up to enjoy all the good things the day will bring. God invites you to release every worry and stress into His care. Let the Lord be the one to figure out the details. Trust Him to fix the chaotic circumstances for your good and His glory. When it comes down to it, there's nothing you can do that He can't do better.

God cares for you so deeply, friend. He didn't design you to carry the burden alone. He understands the limits you face and where your breaking point is. And because of God's unmatched love, He promises to lift the load off your shoulders so you're free to live with passion and purpose. You'll have margin to love others. And your heart won't become hardened and will instead stay tender to the needs around you.

....

....

....

....

....

....

....

....

....

God, I'm leaving my worries and stresses with You because I can't carry the weight of them any longer. In Jesus' name. Amen.

Be Alert

Be well balanced and always alert, because your enemy, the devil,
roams around incessantly, like a roaring lion looking for its prey to devour.
1 PETER 5:8 TPT

The quickest way to ruin a beautiful day is to let your guard down. Scripture tells us to be alert because the enemy is always looking for ways to bring chaos and panic into your life. And when your faith falters, you're a sitting duck.

This isn't meant to scare you or create anxiety. Instead, let it be a powerful reminder of the believer's battle plan. God wants us to stay connected to Him through time in the Word and in prayer. Starting each day in His glorious presence helps put a hedge of protection around us so we're not easily duped by the devil. Ask God for the spirit of discernment so you can see each situation with truth. And ask for contentment and peace to enjoy every day with eyes wide open.

....

....

....

....

....

....

....

....

....

God, help me be alert so I avoid being fooled by the enemy.
And at the same time, let me live with happiness knowing
You're my protector. In Jesus' name. Amen.

It's by Grace Alone

For by grace you have been saved by faith. Nothing you did could ever earn this salvation, for it was the love gift from God that brought us to Christ! So no one will ever be able to boast, for salvation is never a reward for good works or human striving.
EPHESIANS 2:8–9 TPT

What a relief to know our salvation is *not* dependent on our actions. Truth is, none of us would make it into eternity if left to our own devices. Amen? Nothing unclean or unholy can be in the presence of God. This means our sinful nature disqualifies us, which is why God sent Jesus to pay the price of redemption. His blood made us clean and presentable. And so, it's by God's grace that we've been saved. This should put a huge smile on your face.

Every day, let thankfulness be what drives you to pursue righteousness. Not because it gets you into heaven, but because it points to God's hand in your life. And who knows? That might be the exact reason someone chooses to become a believer.

....

....

....

....

....

....

....

....

....

God, thank You for Your grace. In Jesus' name. Amen.

Don't Partner with the Lies

For we are the product of His hand, heaven's poetry etched on lives, created in the Anointed, Jesus, to accomplish the good works God arranged long ago.
EPHESIANS 2:10 VOICE

The world is full of opportunities to get tangled up in untruths that make us doubt our goodness. We feel unseen and unheard. Maybe our marriage failed or we were let go from our job. Maybe we sit at home every weekend just hoping for an invitation. Or maybe we've failed at something important. Life has a way of punching us in the gut and leaving us feeling worthless.

It's time to stop partnering with these lies. We've done it for far too long. We keep circling the mountain, and it's time to move on. Let's choose to break the familiar cycle for good. Friend, part of living a life of faith is embracing the truth of who we are to God. Let the sweet words of today's verse sink into your DNA; then put on a smile, and go out and have your best day!

....

....

....

....

....

....

....

....

....

God, help me choose to believe I am who You say I am and be confident to enjoy life. In Jesus' name. Amen.

Do You Possess These Traits?

For if you possess these traits and multiply them, then you will never be ineffective or unproductive in your relationship with our Lord Jesus the Anointed; but if you don't have these qualities, then you will be nearsighted and blind, forgetting that your past sins have been washed away.
2 PETER 1:8–9 VOICE

The "traits" referenced above are virtue, faith, knowledge, discipline, endurance, godliness, affection for others, and love. We should strive toward these traits through faith. They're not easy, and most certainly require daily help from God to walk them out well. But having them keeps us on the right path of doing good things for the kingdom and building our relationship with God. Without them, faith will falter, and we'll embrace a life of unrepentant sin. . .again.

Today, take inventory of these traits in yourself. What do they look like in your life? Are there things you need to change? Do you need God's help in certain areas? When you're living a righteous life, it bleeds into everything you do. It's beautiful. And it's God's desire for your life.

....

....

....

....

....

....

God, grow these traits in me until they're mature and strong. In Jesus' name. Amen.

Craving His Presence More Than Money

Keep your lives free from the love of money, and be content with what you have because He has said, "I will never leave you; I will always be by your side."
HEBREWS 13:5 VOICE

There's nothing wrong with having money; it's how we make all the ends meet. And God decides who has it in abundance and who lives on a paycheck-to-paycheck schedule. The problem comes when we *crave* it. When money becomes an idol we worship, it becomes an issue. When we're always wanting more, discontented with our current situation, it's unhealthy. But, friend, there's something that satisfies better than money. It's knowing God's presence is with you always.

Think about it. The God of creation hangs out with you. The one who traveled with the Israelites in the wilderness never leaves your side. The God who gave Noah building plans, who instructed the fish to swallow Jonah, and the one who hung on the cross spends every second in your presence. That makes every day the best day ever!

....

....

....

....

....

....

....

God, let me always crave Your presence over money. In Jesus' name. Amen.

Why Our Weakness Is Good

But he answered me, "My grace is always more than enough
for you, and my power finds its full expression through your
weakness." So I will celebrate my weaknesses, for when I'm weak
I sense more deeply the mighty power of Christ living in me.

2 CORINTHIANS 12:9 TPT

It seems counterintuitive to celebrate our weaknesses. Why would we revel in falling short? Why rejoice over our failures? And why would we applaud not being strong enough to get through our day? But looking through the lens of faith reveals something so magnificent. It shows that when we feel weak, we're able to feel the mighty power of the Lord in us. Our weaknesses are cause for celebration.

If you'll let it, this revelation will free you up to live with abandon. You will enjoy life more because you won't be trying to be someone you're not. It won't upset you to make mistakes. And you'll get a free pass off the performance treadmill. So celebrate weakness because in it you'll experience a deeper awareness of God.

....

....

....

....

....

....

....

God, I'm grateful that my weakness doesn't disqualify me but instead
allows Your power to flow through me. In Jesus' name. Amen.

God Knows

So God knows how to rescue the godly from evil trials. And he knows
how to hold the feet of the wicked to the fire until Judgment Day.
2 PETER 2:9 MSG

"God knows." Those two words are the best day-makers! Why? Because they take the pressure off you trying to figure things out on your own. When the battle is thick, look to God to pull you through. When the grief is heavy, God knows how to bring relief. When you feel surrounded by the enemy, God will keep you from being crushed. He knows how to rescue you.

As a believer, God is your advocate no matter what the day brings your way. Be it trouble, trials, or temptations, He knows what He's doing. So take the pressure off yourself and let God be God. This powerful promise blesses the heart of those in the faith and builds a testimony of His goodness to share with those around you.

God, I don't have to be in control, because You know the ins
and outs of every situation that comes my way. Please rescue
me by Your mighty hand. In Jesus' name. Amen.

The Rich Knowledge of God

May grace and perfect peace cascade over you as you live in
the rich knowledge of God and of Jesus our Lord.
2 PETER 1:2 TPT

Your best day starts by spending time with God first. To acknowledge Him in the morning helps prepare you to weather any storms that come your way. His mercies are new. Your heart is full. You've spent time in prayer—confessing, asking, and praising. And God's Word is like armor, covering you in powerful truths. You are ready for anything.

This is how you live in the rich knowledge of the Lord, because growing your faith takes concerted time and effort. It's choosing to be disciplined. And it's not driven by legalism but by a deep love of God. You just want to know Him better. With each step toward the Lord, you'll experience grace and peace in abundance. That's why your days can be great even if messy.

....

....

....

....

....

....

....

....

....

God, I want to have rich knowledge of You. I want my faith
to grow and mature every day. Place in my heart a deep
desire to know You better. In Jesus' name. Amen.

When You Feel Forgotten

*You are not forgotten, for you have been chosen and destined by Father God.
The Holy Spirit has set you apart to be God's holy ones, obedient followers
of Jesus Christ who have been gloriously sprinkled with his blood. May
God's delightful grace and peace cascade over you many times over!*

1 PETER 1:2 TPT

It's hard to be confident when you feel tossed aside. The reality is, we want to be loved. We want to be cherished. We want to be noticed and seen and heard. We want our thoughts and feelings to matter. We want to be pursued. And when we feel forgotten—especially by those we care about—it affects us. It manifests as bitterness, timidity, or depression. Regardless, it's brutal on our hearts.

That's why today's verse is so wonderful! Even though you feel forgotten, God says you're chosen. Friend, you've been set apart to be His. In the big picture, it doesn't matter what the world thinks, because its Creator sees your immeasurable value. Let this be the foundation of your confidence. Now go out and shine!

God, thank You! In Jesus' name. Amen.

Speaking Blessings Instead

Never retaliate when someone treats you wrongly, nor insult those who insult you, but instead, respond by speaking a blessing over them—because a blessing is what God promised to give you.

1 PETER 3:9 TPT

Yes, the Bible does address those revenge temptations we feel as women. And honestly, we should be glad, because there's nothing more dangerous than a woman poked and prodded at the wrong time. There are times dark clouds roll in to replace once-blue skies, causing our days to take a turn for the worse. It's in these moments that we have a snap choice to make. And if our hearts aren't steeped in God's Word, our fleshly desire to retaliate in kind will prevail.

Time spent with the Lord allows us to take a deep breath when we've been wronged. Mature faith keeps us from insulting back. Why? Because we'll remember God's promised blessing. Choosing to love the unlovable and forgive the unforgivable is rewarded. The clouds won't be able to cover the blue skies, because our days won't be ruined by mean-spiritedness.

....

....

....

....

....

....

....

....

God, help me bless rather than curse every time. In Jesus' name. Amen.

It's the Root

For the love of money—and what it can buy—is the root of all sorts of evil. Some already have wandered away from the true faith because they craved what it had to offer; but when reaching for the prize, they found their hands and hearts pierced with many sorrows.

1 TIMOTHY 6:10 VOICE

Craving what money has to offer is a road that leads to nowhere. Scripture really says that loving money is where all kinds of evil start. We take our eyes off what's *holy* and place our focus on earthly things, which are *holey*. Any pleasure earthly things bring eventually begins to leak out until our hearts are empty once again. Money and what it buys cannot satisfy for long. And we often compromise what we know is right because of it.

Keep your eyes on the prize of eternity every day. Let your heart be filled with godly pursuits, making certain your priorities align with those God blesses. The goal isn't to be rich with earthly treasures but rather to be rich in eternal ones.

....

....

....

....

....

....

....

....

....

God, keep my eyes on what's holy. In Jesus' name. Amen.

It's Time to
Stand Victorious

Now my beloved ones, I have saved these most important truths for last:
Be supernaturally infused with strength through your life-union with the Lord Jesus.
Stand victorious with the force of his explosive power flowing in and through you.
EPHESIANS 6:10 TPT

As a believer, you have everything you need to stand victorious. Gone are the days where you give up and feel defeated. No more wallowing in self-pity, playing the victim. Replaying the offenses over and over again in your mind needs to stop. Friend, you're supernaturally infused with strength because of Jesus. No matter what you face in life, you can handle it.

It's time to rise up and embrace your God-given gifts. You may have a life full of excuses, but they're null and void once you accept Jesus as your Savior. Through Him, you have explosive power flowing in and through you. So be bold in your faith, and live with passion and purpose, trusting He'll give you everything you need to fulfill your calling.

....

....

....

....

....

....

....

God, I know it's time to stand victorious. Help me embrace this
beautiful blessing every day of my life. In Jesus' name. Amen.

Armor Up!

And this is why you need to be head-to-toe in the full armor of God: so you can resist during these evil days and be fully prepared to hold your ground.
EPHESIANS 6:13 VOICE

It's not a stretch of the imagination to believe we're in "these evil days." We're witnessing things we never thought we would see in our lifetimes. We're watching the breakdown of the family unit in epic proportions. We've been in the process of removing God from our schools and government, with more removals coming. We are seeing that right is wrong and wrong is right—and it's causing confusion and chaos. And we often feel powerless to speak out for fear of being canceled.

Friend, the world isn't falling apart; it's falling into place. These things *must* happen according to God's Word. This is why it's vital to put on the full armor of God every day. So spend time with the Lord, armor up, put on your smile, and go be the light of the world.

....

....

....

....

....

....

....

....

God, I appreciate You being my protector and providing the armor I need to face every day with confidence and courage. In Jesus' name. Amen.

Pray Always

Pray always. Pray in the Spirit. Pray about everything in every way you
know how! And keeping all this in mind, pray on behalf of God's people.
Keep on praying feverishly, and be on the lookout until evil has been stayed.
EPHESIANS 6:18 VOICE

Today's verse gives a crystal-clear command for every believer, and it's to be
a prayer warrior. We're to take prayer seriously and make it count. It's not a
once-and-done event. Instead, it's a commitment to take our challenges and
struggles right to God. It's an investment in our relationship with the Father,
and it's a continual conversation.

So, friend, *pray*! Pray about everything that lands on your heart—the good,
the bad, and the ugly. Pray for your needs; pray for your friends and family; pray
for your city and nation; and pray for God's people across the world. Inviting
God into your day will create a joy and peace unmatched by anything else.

....

....

....

....

....

....

....

....

....

God, I love that I can talk directly to You through prayer
anytime and anywhere. Thank You for wanting to hear
the details of my life. In Jesus' name. Amen.

The Devil's Schemes

Put on the full armor of God to protect yourselves
from the devil and his evil schemes.
EPHESIANS 6:11 VOICE

The enemy is always looking for a way to cause trouble and heartache. He walks the perimeter of your life, looking for the cracks and openings, always planning opportunities to bring destruction. His plans for you are never good. That's why God—in His great love and compassion—tells us to put on His full armor.

Where are you the most vulnerable right now? Is it in relationships or finances? Is it in parenting your kids or navigating the aging process with your own parents? Are your emotions high and your ability to trust God low? Talk to Him about these things, and then resolve to armor up every day. And know that no matter what the devil's schemes are, God will *always* use them for your good. So keep your chin up and stay positive. The Lord is with you and for you!

....

....

....

....

....

....

....

....

....

God, it settles my spirit to know You'll always use the
enemy's plans for my benefit and Your glory. You really
do think of everything. In Jesus' name. Amen.

Not Flesh and Blood Alone

We're not waging war against enemies of flesh and blood alone.
No, this fight is against tyrants, against authorities, against supernatural
powers and demon princes that slither in the darkness of this world,
and against wicked spiritual armies that lurk about in heavenly places.
EPHESIANS 6:12 VOICE

When someone makes a rude comment, shakes their fist in anger, or mocks you in public, take a deep breath. When your friend betrays you, your child constantly disobeys you, or your husband leaves you, ask God for a behind-the-scenes reveal of what's going on. While their actions cut deep, the enemy isn't the person standing in front of you. Instead, scripture clearly says our fight is also in the spiritual realm.

Of course, there are natural consequences to their actions. But it's important to remember we have an enemy looking to destroy and devour, and he will use others to help his cause. So ask God every day for discernment and wisdom to know who your enemy is—and who your enemy is not. Let Him offer perspective, give direction, and bring healing.

....

....

....

....

....

....

....

God, I'm so grateful You see everything and know
everything. In Jesus' name. Amen.

The Magnificence of God

"Rescue us every time we face tribulation and set us free from evil.
For you are the King who rules with power and glory forever. Amen."
MATTHEW 6:13 TPT

Start your day by acknowledging the magnificence of God. Meditate on the goodness you have seen from Him in your life and in the lives of those you love. Let God know how much you appreciate His unwavering compassion. Recognize the Lord's sovereignty. Show gratitude for the ways He equips you to navigate the ups and downs of life. And thank God for His unmatched power and glory and how He blesses you through them.

This act of worship sets your heart right. It reminds you of His awesomeness—of all the times He followed through. So, when the trials and tribulations come throughout the day, you're already bathed in His Truth. You trust God for a rescue. And the enemy's plans to harm you will fall short.

....

....

....

....

....

....

....

....

....

God, I love to think back to the ways You have saved me and restored me. You are indeed magnificent! I trust You to rescue me from every evil, every time. In Jesus' name. Amen.

Surrendering Anxiety

Surrender your anxiety. Be still and realize that I am God. I am God above all the nations, and I am exalted throughout the whole earth.
PSALM 46:10 TPT

Don't let worry and anxiety ruin your day. Because they will. Chances are, they already have at some point. And sometimes we don't even realize we're drowning in our worries. For many, anxiety is a constant companion and the lens we view our lives through. And God wants us to surrender it all.

When we hold on to anxiety, we're essentially telling the Lord we don't need help. We're choosing not to trust His power and might in our circumstances. And we're letting our worry ruin the life we were created to live. It does nothing but suck the energy and enjoyment out of your day. Friend, let God be God. Ask Him to intervene in meaningful ways, filling you with peace so your heart can be free to live and love well!

....
....
....
....
....
....
....
....

God, I confess I've held on to anxiety instead of trusting You, and I can't do it any longer. Help me release my worries into Your capable hands, knowing You'll free me to live untangled. In Jesus' name. Amen.

A Proven Help

God, you're such a safe and powerful place to find refuge! You're a proven help in time of trouble—more than enough and always available whenever I need you.
PSALM 46:1 TPT

It's a blessing to serve a God who's always available. Be it two in the morning or two in the afternoon, the Lord is ready and willing to hear you and help you. Sometimes we may think our most pressing need is too insignificant to bring to God. We worry He has bigger fish to fry, and our request will be nothing of importance. But that simply isn't good theology.

God is omnipresent and omnipotent, which means He's ever-present and all-powerful. He can give full attention to everyone at the same time. So, when you need a safe and powerful place of refuge or help in troubling times, pray. You'll have a private audience with Him! Tell God exactly what you need. Because, without fail, He has a perfect track record in your life. He is a proven help!

....

....

....

....

....

....

....

....

....

God, when I'm in the middle of the mess, remind me
You're my proven help. In Jesus' name. Amen.

Unerodable Faith

So we will never fear even if every structure of support were to crumble away. We will not fear even when the earth quakes and shakes, moving mountains and casting them into the sea. For the raging roar of stormy winds and crashing waves cannot erode our faith in you.
PSALM 46:2–3 TPT

Let this declaration be yours! You have a purpose on planet earth, and fear has potential to ruin it. Every day is an opportunity to promote the name of Jesus. Being afraid will keep you from it. And if you allow fear to discourage and depress you, your testimony will suffer. You get to choose whether you live in victory or defeat. It's up to you whether your days are good or bad.

Ask God to give you the kind of faith that won't erode when the winds and waves hit. Be unshakable in your belief that He will come through. When you feel the quakes and shakes begin, let God straighten your back as you stand strong. When life starts to crumble, let God strengthen your structure of trust. Fear not, my friend.

....

....

....

....

....

....

....

....

....

God, make my faith unerodable! In Jesus' name. Amen.

God Is Able

Come, gaze, fix your eyes on what the Eternal can do. Amazing, He has worked desolation here on this battlefield, earth. God can stop wars anywhere in the world. He can make scrap of all weapons: snap bows, shatter spears, and burn shields.
PSALM 46:8–9 VOICE

If God can stop wars anywhere in the world, He can change the trajectory of your day. If He can make scrap of weapons, He can intervene when your circumstances start going south. God can stop the arguments birthed from hard conversations. He can shift your mood with the snap of a finger. Nothing in your day is too big for Him.

So, knowing that, focus your eyes on God. Be quick to cry out for His help at the first sign of trouble. The Lord understands the forces coming against you, and He knows what needs to happen next. To try and figure things out for yourself is counterproductive especially because God is able and willing to step in and bring resolution right now.

....

....

....

....

....

....

....

....

God, I appreciate You knowing the ins and outs of every situation I face. Let me always submit to Your authority. In Jesus' name. Amen.

Contentment

You see we came into this world with nothing, and nothing is going with us on the way out! So as long as we are clothed and fed, we should be happy.
1 Timothy 6:7–8 voice

We have every reason to be content, yet sometimes we forget. We forget God is all we need because He provides for our needs. We forget we're merely passing through on our way to eternity, so this world holds no value in our hearts. We forget we don't have to keep up with the trends and make bank to be happy. Simply put, we forget who God is to us. And we've all done it at one time or another.

Every day, let's live with contented hearts. Let's find joy in the little things. Let's remember nothing earthly compares to what's heavenly. And let's remember we came into this world with nothing, and we're leaving with the same. That frees us up to look for our contentment in God alone. Living with that mindset will make for beautiful days ahead!

....

....

....

....

....

....

....

....

....

God, my contentment is found in You alone! In Jesus' name. Amen.

Crushed Places

Purify my conscience! Make this leper clean again! Wash me in your love until I am pure in heart. Satisfy me in your sweetness, and my song of joy will return. The places you have crushed within me will rejoice in your healing touch.

PSALM 51:7–8 TPT

We all need to have God crush places within us. There's sin that needs to be smashed into dust so it can blow away in the wind. We need certain streams of thought chased out. And God is the one we can trust to set things right in us. Any hard work the Lord does to bring renewal is done in love. He purifies in a way that leaves us feeling validated and worthy. There's peace through the process. God is the only one able to clean us up with graciousness.

Invite the Lord to wash you clean in His love until your heart is pure. God wants your heart! And if you surrender every day in faith, you'll experience joy and peace this world cannot replicate.

God, crush those places in me that keep me from the fullness of life in You. In Jesus' name. Amen.

God Will Provide for You

God provides for His own. It is pointless to get up early,
work hard, and go to bed late anxiously laboring for food to eat;
for God provides for those He loves, even while they are sleeping.
PSALM 127:2 VOICE

This verse brings comfort, especially for those of us who constantly feel over-whelmed to make ends meet. Many of us work ourselves to the bone, feeling pressure to provide. And, rather than enjoy the ones we love, we burn the candle at both ends, missing out on sweet community. Even more, we miss out on watching God's faithfulness in action.

God provides for those who love Him. He promises to watch over you, friend. Every day, He will meet your needs—both spoken and unspoken. And scripture says it's pointless to strive so hard when your heavenly Father has everything in motion. God is at work in your life every moment of every day. Let this beautiful truth reduce your stress level so you can be present with friends and family. God's got you.

....
....
....
....
....
....
....
....

God, help me relax and trust that You know my needs
and will meet them. In Jesus' name. Amen.

Workplace Attitudes

Instruct every employee to respect and honor their employers, for this attitude presents to them a clear testimony of God's truth and renown. Tell them to never provide them with a reason to discredit God's name because of their actions.
1 TIMOTHY 6:1 TPT

It matters how you act in the workplace, especially when your coworkers know you're a believer. Just as your life preaches when you are out and about with family and friends, it also preaches when you are at work. You may not agree with the decisions of your supervisor or certain company policies, but scripture says to respect and honor them anyway. Because when you do, your actions will speak volumes of God's influence in your life.

Be a light at work. Bring joy to the job. Every day, show positivity and kindness to others. Model a generous spirit to those in authority. And let honesty and integrity guide the way you conduct yourself.

....

....

....

....

....

....

....

....

....

God, help me remember that I can change the tone at work by how I conduct myself. Every chance I get, let me make the workplace better as I honor You with my actions. In Jesus' name. Amen.

Deep in Your Heart

So if you believe deep in your heart that God raised Jesus from the pit of death and if you voice your allegiance by confessing the truth that "Jesus is Lord," then you will be saved! Belief begins in the heart and leads to a life that's right with God; confession departs from our lips and brings eternal salvation.
ROMANS 10:9–10 VOICE

Let your daily confession be proof you have faith deep in your heart. Any chance you get, proclaim the name of Jesus to those who will listen. You don't have to stand on the street corner with signage or go door-to-door, handing out pamphlets. But be ready to share God's goodness when the divine door of opportunity opens. Ask the Lord to give you the right words, at the right time, to speak in the right way to the right people.

And always make sure your heart is right with God by confessing and repenting. Soak yourself in God's Word daily, letting scripture marinate your mind. These are faith-building activities that will produce a deeper faith in your spirit each day.

God, I believe deep in my heart! In Jesus' name. Amen.

When You Try to Outdo

Be devoted to tenderly loving your fellow believers as members of one family. Try to outdo yourselves in respect and honor of one another.

ROMANS 12:10 TPT

If you must try and outdo others, then be better at loving. Have more compassion. Be more generous with your time and treasure. If (in your mind) it's a competition, then compete for having the most surrendered servant's heart. Work to be more gracious and giving. Be more devoted to your community and your God. Respect others more. Honor those around you better.

Choosing to have tender love for fellow believers is a beautiful decision because it blesses the body as a whole. It's God's command. And when you are willing to show this kind of compassion, it will be returned. Scripture shares countless examples of the concept of sowing and reaping. So let the Lord infiltrate your heart every day so it's ready to embrace others with gusto and receive the same in return.

....

....

....

....

....

....

....

....

God, I do have a competitive nature, and I'm grateful Your Word addresses how to focus it on tenderly loving others with passion and purpose. In Jesus' name. Amen.

Bless Instead of Curse

Ironically this same tongue can be both an instrument of blessing to our Lord and Father and a weapon that hurls curses upon others who are created in God's own image. One mouth streams forth both blessings and curses. My brothers and sisters, this is not how it should be.

JAMES 3:9–10 VOICE

Friend, does this verse shine a spotlight on your life? The truth is, we can use our words to encourage a downtrodden friend in one moment and an hour later verbally berate another for being annoying. We can deliver words of kindness and then yell at a frustrating driver only minutes apart. Unfortunately, our mouths can do both without a second thought.

Consider this a challenge to be different. Let every day be an opportunity to shine caring and compassionate words into a hurting world. Be thoughtful in what you say, choosing to keep silent rather than be cruel. Leave somebody better than you found them. Be charitable with compliments and affirmations.

....

....

....

....

....

....

....

....

God, I confess I've used words to hurt others. Help me to bless instead of curse, glorifying You in the process. In Jesus' name. Amen.

We Are Different by Design

Whenever you're trying to look better than others or get the better of others, things fall apart and everyone ends up at the others' throats.
JAMES 3:16 MSG

There's so much wisdom in the above verse that we can apply to our everyday interactions. If our goal is to thrive in life and get along with others, then there's no place for any feelings of superiority. You are no better than anyone else, because we are all God's children. And because He made each of us to be unique and special, being different is by design—it's on purpose. The world may encourage you to feel *better than* or *less than* but following this recipe will only alienate you from much-needed community.

Find beauty in the uniqueness of your friends, and cheer them on in their own journeys! Instead of comparing yourself to others, let God bring a spirit of unity into your heart. And when jealousy rears its ugly head, squash it through prayer. There simply isn't room in your day for that kind of distraction.

....

....

....

....

....

....

....

....

....

God, thank You for making us different. Help me to see the beauty in all Your creation. In Jesus' name. Amen.

Why We Need Community

*You can develop a healthy, robust community that lives right with
God and enjoy its results only if you do the hard work of getting along
with each other, treating each other with dignity and honor.*
JAMES 3:18 MSG

Community is such a vital part of a believer's life. We need one another to
walk it well. Amen? We need to be held accountable. We need people to come
alongside us in support. And it's in community where we develop a servant's
heart for helping those around us. But it's hard work to love in such a way.

Ask God to give you a willing spirit so you can treat others with dignity
and honor. Ask Him to give you a love for those who are often unlovable,
incentivizing you to get along with each other. And let God give you vision
for the future so you understand the need for a strong and loving community.
Done right, community can turn a bad day into a good one by simply linking
arms in solidarity.

....

....

....

....

....

....

....

....

....

*God, help me find a community of believers to
grow with. In Jesus' name. Amen.*

Your Faith Pleases God

It's impossible to please God apart from faith. And why?
Because anyone who wants to approach God must believe both that he
exists and that he cares enough to respond to those who seek him.

HEBREWS 11:6 MSG

It's hard to imagine not following the Lord. Chances are you've seen His hand move in your life countless times. God is why you have hope in your marriage. Faith is why you take steps out of your comfort zone. It's why you extend grace, forgiving those who've hurt you. It's why you spend time in God's Word and in prayer. And every time your faith is activated, be assured your Father in heaven is delighted.

So let others see the way you love God. Live with authenticity every day, always ready to share your testimony when the Holy Spirit prompts you. Who knows? . . . You might be the reason someone chooses to become a believer. You might be why they come to faith, pleasing God with their decision to follow Him.

God, it delights my heart to know my faith delights Yours. Help me
make choices today that glorify You. In Jesus' name. Amen.

Choosing Peace

Listen, don't get trapped in brainless debates; avoid competition over family trees or pedigrees; stay away from fights and disagreements over the law. They are a waste of your time.
TITUS 3:9 VOICE

Can't we just all get along? Have you ever felt this way? Maybe it's heated discussions over a family dinner. Maybe it's difficult parents on your child's sports team. Maybe it's your coworkers who can't seem to agree on a direction for the project. Or maybe it's your in-laws, always critical of everything you do. God's Word directly addresses discord and conflict, reminding us they are a waste of time.

Friend, always choose the path of peace. We don't have to speak every thought that crosses our minds. We don't have to respond to every prodding. And we don't need to one-up others. There's nothing constructive or beneficial in doing so. And even when engaged in difficult but necessary conversations, our spirit can be settled. Let peace reign in your heart so it reigns in your day as well!

....

....

....

....

....

....

....

God, give me self-control to keep my mouth shut rather than join in time-wasting discussions. Help me choose the path of peace instead. In Jesus' name. Amen.

The Power of Words

Don't tear down another person with your words. Instead, keep the
peace, and be considerate. Be truly humble toward everyone.
TITUS 3:2 VOICE

One way to ensure a good day is to be careful with your words because they
have power to pull someone out of the pit of depression or put them there.
They bring healing or cause harm. With them, you can stir up chaos or usher
in peace. Words can be spoken in humility, creating a sweet environment, or
they can repel others with prideful boasting.

As you think back over the week, have your words blessed others and
glorified God? Have you been considerate and thoughtful even when saying
hard things? Did you look for opportunities to encourage? Or have you been
reckless, using words as weapons out of frustration or anger? Everyone's in a
battle somewhere in their life. Knowing that, let every day be a golden opportunity to be kind and generous with the words you speak.

....

....

....

....

....

....

....

....

God, I confess the times I've used words irresponsibly.
Help me show compassion in my speech so others
feel loved and valued. In Jesus' name. Amen.

Taking a Stand

If a person is causing divisions in the community, warn him once;
and if necessary, warn him twice. After that, avoid him completely
because by then you are sure that you are dealing with a corrupt,
sinful person. He is determined to condemn himself.

TITUS 3:10–11 VOICE

It's hard to be around negative people who are always stirring up trouble. They have a special way of ruining a good day because their pessimism kills the mood. They take sides and cause stress in community; and God's Word says to address it with them. *Twice.* Then, if nothing changes, His command is to avoid that relationship, so your heart isn't corrupted by their cynicism.

Yes, confrontation can be uncomfortable, so ask the Lord to give you the right words to speak with confidence. Understand that your boldness in those difficult moments is obedience. And, as we read throughout God's Word, obeying reaps rewards. So take a stand because it's God's desire for you and for the one causing division.

....

....

....

....

....

....

....

....

God, thank You for addressing pessimism in Your Word.
It's hard to be around negativity. Give me courage to obey
and take a stand. In Jesus' name. Amen.

The Wisdom of Older Women

And here's what I want you to teach the older women: Be respectful. Steer clear of gossip or drinking too much so that you can teach what is good to young women. Be a positive example, showing them what it is to love their husbands and children, and teaching them to control themselves in every way and to be pure.

TITUS 2:3–5 VOICE

Because being older provides a platform to encourage younger people, be mindful to let your love of God shine in all you do. There's a grace that comes with age, giving us a different perspective on life. We've collected hard-won wisdom along the way. We've been through the battles and have seen God's mighty hand at work. We've lived long enough to understand how life ebbs and flows as we trust His will and ways. We have had husbands and raised kids and learned tough lessons because of it. So be an encourager for younger women who need hope.

Let them see your faith in action. Show them righteous living. And teach them to live joyous days in His presence!

....

....

....

....

....

....

....

....

God, use me! In Jesus' name. Amen.

Running Away

Grace arrives with its own instruction: run away from anything that leads us away from God; abandon the lusts and passions of this world; live life now in this age with awareness and self-control, doing the right thing and keeping yourselves holy.
TITUS 2:12 VOICE

It's interesting to note scripture says to "run" from whatever leads us away from God. It doesn't tell us to simply turn our backs or try to avoid it. It doesn't say to walk in the opposite direction. Instead, it's telling us to hightail it out of there. This should capture our attention!

Pursuing a righteous life takes intentionality. It requires you to make hard choices in the moment. And it means that you release the lusts and passions that have driven you in the past and choose instead to do the right things. It's valuing holiness over happiness. Every day is a journey of faith meant to be enjoyed when you let God direct your path!

....

....

....

....

....

....

....

....

....

God, open my eyes to see the temptations that lead me away
from You, then give me the good mind to run from them
and into Your arms. In Jesus' name. Amen.

God's Not a Liar

We rest in this hope we've been given—the hope that we will live forever with our God—the hope that He proclaimed ages and ages ago (even before time began). And our God is no liar; He is not even capable of uttering lies.
TITUS 1:2 VOICE

It's so comforting to know that God is incapable of lying. His promises are unbreakable. His vision for our future is unshakable. And His hope for us is unwavering. Do you recognize the privilege you have to be counted as one chosen by God? There are many who have turned their backs on Him, but not you. You've been able to find rest and peace, knowing you'll live forever with the Lord.

So, friend, let every day be a celebration! Even in those tough moments and disappointing seasons, let the depth of your faith give you reason to rejoice. This life will bring heartbreak, but God has promised restoration. You may be broken, but He promises healing. And God doesn't lie.

God, I appreciate that You are true to Your Word. And I love that every promise made is a promise kept. In Jesus' name. Amen.

Choosing Faith Over Fear

For God will never give you the spirit of fear, but the Holy Spirit
who gives you mighty power, love, and self-control.
2 TIMOTHY 1:7 TPT

Your best life does not include being gripped by the spirit of fear. While there may be a million reasons for it, God has given each believer the Holy Spirit to counteract any fearful responses to unsettling circumstances. You've been given mighty power to keep moving forward. In addition, you have love, keeping your heart tender and connected to God. And the Spirit also gives self-control, which helps you keep emotions in check. So any fear that brings a sense of dread or steals your peace isn't from God.

Friend, it's time to embrace this beautiful gift of faith over fear. It's a choice to not walk the route of fear when it presents itself. It takes intentionality to choose to trust God instead. But when you do, the Spirit floods you with power, love, and self-control to stand strong. Every day, you can live in freedom and victory!

God, I want to continually choose faith over fear so I can
live the life You've created for me. In Jesus' name. Amen.

Legacy of Faith

As I think of your strong faith that was passed down through your family line. It began with your grandmother Lois, who passed it on to your dear mother, Eunice. And it's clear that you too are following in the footsteps of their godly example.
2 TIMOTHY 1:5 TPT

One of the reasons we want to live each day to its fullest potential is because we know little eyes are watching us. Whether we're a mother, a spiritual mother, an aunt, a teacher, or a family friend, we have the privilege of influencing the next generation of believers. The way we live our lives might be the catalyst to someone's choice to follow the Lord.

Be thoughtful with how you live each day. The way you react to the ups and downs of life can deeply affect how others view God. Through your responses, they will either see a woman of faith or a woman of fear. They will see a surrendered heart or stubbornness. Ask God for the confidence to live your faith out loud, knowing it's a testimony to His goodness.

....

....

....

....

....

....

....

....

....

God, help me create a legacy of faith. In Jesus' name. Amen.

You're Old Enough

And don't let anyone put you down because you're young. Teach believers
with your life: by word, by demeanor, by love, by faith, by integrity.
1 TIMOTHY 4:12 MSG

If you're a young woman who doesn't feel old enough to be a voice of faith to the community, let today's verse be an encouragement to you! God calls women *of all ages* to share His Word and their testimony. No matter how old you are, there's a God-given call on your life, and He will activate it at the perfect time. You can trust that promise.

Begin every day by telling God, *yes.* Even if He's asking you to do something that could make you anxious or be a big step out of your comfort zone, let Him know you will obey. Confirm you're ready and willing to go wherever He leads. Be intentional to grow your faith and deepen your relationship with the Lord. And remember your life always preaches by the choices you make—whether on the sidelines or in the game. Live each day with love and integrity!

....

....

....

....

....

....

....

....

....

God, my answer to You is a resounding yes! I am
ready and willing. In Jesus' name. Amen.

God-Breathed

All of Scripture is God-breathed; in its inspired voice, we hear useful teaching, rebuke, correction, instruction, and training for a life that is right so that God's people may be up to the task ahead and have all they need to accomplish every good work.

2 TIMOTHY 3:16–17 VOICE

Don't listen to those who discredit the Bible. Some say it's just a bunch of outdated and irrelevant stories. Some think it's only partly true. And still some say it's not divinely inspired, flawed by human authors. As believers, we simply can't give credibility to any of these claims because we know the truth.

The Bible is alive and active. It's how God reveals Himself to those who love Him. And if God says it's divinely inspired, then by faith we believe it. Think back to the times God spoke to you through a verse or when His Word brought comfort and peace. Hold those times close to your heart so nothing can sway you to doubt.

....

....

....

....

....

....

....

....

God, I'm so grateful for the Bible. I believe it in full, from Genesis to Revelation. Help me guard my heart from anything that might change my belief. In Jesus' name. Amen.

Steer Clear

As the end approaches, people are going to be self-absorbed, money-hungry, self-promoting, stuck-up, profane, contemptuous of parents, crude, coarse, dog-eat-dog, unbending, slanderers, impulsively wild, savage, cynical, treacherous, ruthless, bloated windbags, addicted to lust, and allergic to God. They'll make a show of religion, but behind the scenes they're animals. Stay clear of these people.

2 TIMOTHY 3:2–5 MSG

We need God's divine discernment so we don't follow worldly ways. We need vision and strength from Him. We need to actively protect our hearts from being tainted by these impurities. Every day, we need to stand up in faith and refuse to be part of the wickedness and corruption. If our desire is to have the light of Jesus shine within us, then acting in these ways will only extinguish it.

Scripture is crystal clear when it says to steer clear of certain kinds of people. It's not because we are better than they are; it's because our priorities are different than theirs. So, every day, choose to be steeped in the joy of the Lord, and trust the Holy Spirit to guide you on the paths that glorify God.

....

....

....

....

....

....

....

....

....

God, I'm focused on You. In Jesus' name. Amen.

Stubborn Know-It-Alls

We cross the threshold of true knowledge when we live in
obedient devotion to God. Stubborn know-it-alls will never stop
to do this, for they scorn true wisdom and knowledge.

PROVERBS 1:7 TPT

Do you know a stubborn know-it-all? Their demeanor becomes a huge barrier to obedience. Rather than follow God's leading, they decide their way is best. They're unable to hear direction from the Lord because they are convinced it's inferior to the plans they've made. To them, it's their life to live, making it impossible to trust an unknown future to an unseen God.

What's missing is a true understanding of who God is. Know-it-alls don't trust His faithfulness. They can't embrace His love and compassion. They're unwilling to accept God's sovereignty. We may have a track record of good ideas, but our thoughts are not His thoughts. Our ways are not His ways. And that's good news! Even more, scripture confirms that God blesses our obedience. So, every time we surrender, that devotion produces a harvest of good things to come.

....

....

....

....

....

....

....

....

God, soften my heart so I choose Your way over mine—
every time. In Jesus' name. Amen.

Making Every Day Count

And now the time is fast approaching for my release from this life and I am ready to be offered as a sacrifice. I have fought an excellent fight. I have finished my full course with all my might and I've kept my heart full of faith.
2 TIMOTHY 4:6–7 TPT

Paul fully embraced every day of his ministry with passion and purpose. He found joy in every circumstance—even shipwrecks and jail time! He gave it everything he had, pushing forward to spread the gospel to the Gentiles. And it was his heart, full of faith in the Lord, that fueled every step of the way. There's no doubt Paul fought an excellent fight and finished well.

Let Paul's life encourage you. Consider you're here at this time on the kingdom calendar to be a light in this sometimes-dark world. Make each day count! Don't waste time on things that keep you from God—like anger, unforgiveness, pride, and selfishness. Instead, be present and engaged. Shine the awesomeness of God to those around you!

....

....

....

....

....

....

....

....

....

God, let everything in my life preach Your goodness every day! In Jesus' name. Amen.

Solid Biblical Teaching

You're going to find that there will be times when people will have no stomach
for solid teaching, but will fill up on spiritual junk food—catchy opinions
that tickle their fancy. They'll turn their backs on truth and chase mirages.
But you—keep your eye on what you're doing; accept the hard times along
with the good; keep the Message alive; do a thorough job as God's servant.

2 Timothy 4:3–5 MSG

Many argue we're not in these difficult times right now. Rather than seek solid biblical teaching, they want to hear what makes them feel good. They want Christianity-lite. And they expect God to be their genie in the bottle, giving them what they need the moment they ask for it. How shallow.

But not you, friend. You're committed to learning every bit of the Bible— the easy and difficult to hear—because you believe it's complete, instructive, and relevant. You desire the deep waters of faith with God. And you know He's compassionate and trustworthy, and that's why you're able to live every day to its fullest!

....

....

....

....

....

....

....

....

God, help me deepen my faith so it's not
shallow. In Jesus' name. Amen.

Growing Your Faith

Brothers and sisters, we cannot help but thank God for you, which is only appropriate because your faith is growing and expanding and because the love demonstrated by each and every one of you is overflowing for one another.
2 Thessalonians 1:3 voice

Your faith should be growing every day, and that only happens with time invested. Done right, it's evident to those around you. They will see a kinder, gentler you. They'll see humility and a desire to live and love well. They will see it in your choices because every right decision will be pleasing to God. And others will notice the way you care for their hearts in good times and bad.

You have the privilege of knowing God in meaningful ways. Those moments studying scripture deepen your understanding of Him. Those prayerful times connect your heart to His. And, as you grow in your relationship, it will bless you as well as the community of believers around you. Let every day be an opportunity to learn more about your Lord.

....

....

....

....

....

....

....

....

....

God, grow my faith so I can be a light to those around me. In Jesus' name. Amen.

Do It for God

Put your heart and soul into every activity you do, as though
you are doing it for the Lord himself and not merely for others.
For we know that we will receive a reward, an inheritance from
the Lord, as we serve the Lord Yahweh, the Anointed One!
COLOSSIANS 3:23–24 TPT

If you're about to have "one of those days" because what's on the schedule is overwhelming or unenjoyable, why not change your perspective? Decide that what you're about to do will bless God. That it's all for Him. This mindset will allow you to muster a good attitude and a willing spirit to move forward in a productive way. It will turn a potentially bad day into a good one!

Tell God why you're struggling, and ask Him to help get your heart right. Let the Lord encourage your next steps, giving you the energy and wisdom to walk it out well. And remember that your obedience will be rewarded. God will recognize your desire to glorify Him, and you'll be blessed for it.

God, when I'm struggling to do something, remind me that my
obedience delights Your heart. In Jesus' name. Amen.

Tolerating Their Weaknesses

Tolerate the weaknesses of those in the family of faith, forgiving one another in the same way you have been graciously forgiven by Jesus Christ. If you find fault with someone, release this same gift of forgiveness to them. For love is supreme and must flow through each of these virtues. Love becomes the mark of true maturity.
COLOSSIANS 3:13–14 TPT

It's difficult to tolerate weakness in those around you, especially when you're often the one suffering the natural consequences. But when you don't extend grace, it builds up a wall of bitterness in your heart toward them, and you tend to keep score of their wrongs. Since God has commanded us to love and forgive others, how are we able to justify these actions?

Your days will be filled with more joy if you'll choose to release the gift of forgiveness to others—just as the Lord has done for you. No one is perfect, not even you. Ask God to give you tolerance when others fall short. You'll want the same grace extended when you mess up.

....

....

....

....

....

....

....

....

God, teach me to love and forgive quickly and graciously. In Jesus' name. Amen.

Always and Dearly

You are always and dearly loved by God! So robe yourself with virtues of God, since you have been divinely chosen to be holy. Be merciful as you endeavor to understand others, and be compassionate, showing kindness toward all. Be gentle and humble, unoffendable in your patience with others.

<small>COLOSSIANS 3:12 TPT</small>

There is something beautiful that happens to a woman who knows she is *always* and *dearly* loved. It frees her up to live with God-given self-assurance. To know she has been set apart—she's been chosen—speaks volumes into her self-worth. It brings joy into each day, giving her the ability to be full of mercy and compassion toward others. And this confidence keeps her unoffendable because she knows she is God's beloved.

How would your day be different if this described you? Spend time with God today, sharing your thoughts on the paragraph above. Tell Him your heart's desire. If you need to grieve, grieve in His presence. If you need things to shift in your belief system, ask for help. Let God bring this truth into full bloom in your life.

....

....

....

....

....

....

....

....

God, let it be! In Jesus' name. Amen.

The Daily Journey of Faith

*So kill your earthly impulses: loose sex, impure actions, unbridled
sensuality, wicked thoughts, and greed (which is essentially idolatry).
It's because of these that God's wrath is coming [upon the sons
and daughters of disobedience], so avoid them at all costs.*
COLOSSIANS 3:5–6 VOICE

If you're a believer, your best days should be filled with choices that please God.
Your faith should guide with keen discernment, helping you make decisions
that bless and not curse. Done with intention, every path taken will lead to
peace—even when the path is difficult. And old habits will be willingly replaced
by those that reflect your love for God.

Let the Lord strengthen you for the choices ahead. Let Him know where
you're struggling to let go of past behaviors. We all need daily renewal by God
so we can confidently kill the ugly, earthly impulses that have gripped us for
too long. Friend, faith is a daily journey. Hold your Father's hand, and let Him
lead you through it.

....

....

....

....

....

....

....

....

*God, I want my life to look different from what I see
applauded by the world. Help my choices point to my
faith in You. In Jesus' name. Amen.*

We've All Sinned

You see, all have sinned, and all their futile attempts to reach God in His glory fail. Yet they are now saved and set right by His free gift of grace through the redemption available only in Jesus the Anointed.
ROMANS 3:23–24 VOICE

Before we point a finger at somebody else in condemnation, let's remember a powerful truth. We've all sinned—*every single one of us*. And because of that, we've all fallen short of God's glory. We are flawed people, living together in a fallen world, desperate for a Savior. Enter Jesus. . . .

It's because of God's great love and compassion that He sent His one and only Son from a throne in heaven to a cross on Calvary. Christ's death sealed our redemption. It settled our salvation. So let every day be an opportunity to rejoice! In God's unshakable grace, Jesus came to set things right. He is why we'll be in eternity. And when we accept Him as our personal Savior, every day is a celebration.

....

....

....

....

....

....

....

....

....

God, thank You for bridging the gap sin left through the death of Your Son on the cross. What a beautiful gift! In Jesus' name. Amen.

Learning to Be Content

*I am not saying this because I am in need. I have learned to be content
in whatever circumstances. I know how to survive in tight situations,
and I know how to enjoy having plenty. In fact, I have learned how
to face any circumstances: fed or hungry, with or without.*
PHILIPPIANS 4:11–12 VOICE

Your day will be so much more enjoyable if you're able to roll with the punches.
Sometimes our best laid plans change on a dime, so the ability to be flexible is
a blessing! Other times life doesn't turn out the way we'd hoped, and we must
find peace in the chaos anyway. To think life won't throw a curveball is a setup
for irritation and frustration.

Ask God for the gift of contentment each day so you're able to find peace
in every circumstance. He will give you the ability to rise above the choppy
waters so you're not tossed about in the waves. He'll generate in you a sense
of peace the world can't understand. And you'll have a happy heart, satisfied
in the goodness of God.

....

....

....

....

....

....

....

....

....

God, all I need is You! In Jesus' name. Amen.

Your Life Preaches

Keep your gentle nature so that all people will know what it looks like to walk in His footsteps. The Lord is ever present with us.
PHILIPPIANS 4:5 VOICE

Your actions preach either one way or another. Make no mistake. If you profess to be a Christian but you cuss out the waitress because your meal came out cold, others will notice. When you're unwilling to forgive an offense, it will catch their attention. It will be hard to reconcile in their minds because your words and actions won't align.

You have an opportunity every day to highlight the Lord. Even in your imperfections, He can be glorified by how you choose to respond. The Lord can use your life to show His love to those around you. Your kindness and generosity will speak volumes. Let your love for God shine through your life so others will be encouraged to follow Him too.

....
....
....
....
....
....
....
....
....

God, help me be mindful that my life preaches for You or against You. Let my heart be purified through the Word and time with You so what naturally flows from it is glorifying! In Jesus' name. Amen.

Pray Instead

Don't be anxious about things; instead, pray. Pray about everything. He longs to hear your requests, so talk to God about your needs and be thankful for what has come.
PHILIPPIANS 4:6 VOICE

Every good day starts with morning prayer on the front end, divine conversations throughout the day, and a wrap-up prayer as you drift off to sleep. It's that continuous talk with God that helps your heart stay hopeful. The Word says to pray about everything, which means nothing is off-limits. From a good parking place in the rain, to words needed in a hard discussion, to ideas for dinner, you have freedom to converse with God all day long about every single thing. Isn't it wonderful He wants to hear it all?

Let God make your good day a *great* day! Invite Him into your plans as you enjoy His company. Share your anxiety and speak your gratitude. Let God be your listening ear all day long. And watch how others are drawn to your hope-filled attitude, wanting to know more.

....

....

....

....

....

....

....

....

God, be my constant companion and the one I enjoy spending time with the most. In Jesus' name. Amen.

Guarding Your Mind

Finally, brothers and sisters, fill your minds with beauty and truth.
Meditate on whatever is honorable, whatever is right, whatever is pure,
whatever is lovely, whatever is good, whatever is virtuous and praiseworthy.
PHILIPPIANS 4:8 VOICE

In the world we live in today—with bad news coming at us constantly through our devices—it's imperative we regulate what we ingest. When we don't, we end up afraid. We see nothing but horrible outcomes and bad endings ahead. And we let our thoughts run amok. That's a sure way to feel anxious, courtesy of the enemy's playbook.

As believers, we're to fill our minds with other things—things to settle our spirits and quiet our thoughts. When the world feels overwhelming, meditate on things that are praiseworthy. Chew on the good you see happening in your life. Focus on what's pure and lovely. Think of times where truth won and honorable moments unfolded. And every day, fill your mind with beauty and truth so you can be a blessing to the world around you.

....

....

....

....

....

....

....

....

God, help me guard my heart from the bad news of the
world and focus on You instead. In Jesus' name. Amen.

The Problem with Always

*With tender humility and quiet patience, always demonstrate
gentleness and generous love toward one another, especially
toward those who may try your patience.*

EPHESIANS 4:2 TPT

The keyword in today's verse is *always*. Honestly, this is what trips us up because it's hard to be intentional to do anything *always*. Amen? And the idea that we should consistently be gentle and constantly demonstrate generous love toward others feels like a setup for failure. Add to that the command to show this to those who drive us nuts, and you may as well lock us up right now.

But then we remember perfection isn't the goal. In this human condition, it's impossible. Even more, we serve a God who forgives. While we may strive every day to do what God has asked, there will be times we fail miserably. In those moments, we repent, we apologize, and we try again. And then we thank the Lord, because He always loves us—even when we mess up.

*God, help me have tender humility and quiet patience with everybody
so they're able to see You in my actions. In Jesus' name. Amen.*

Perfect Father

For the Lord God is one, and so are we, for we share in one faith,
one baptism, and one Father. And he is the perfect Father who
leads us all, works through us all, and lives in us all!
EPHESIANS 4:5–6 TPT

Many of us did not have loving fathers growing up. They were often sources of deep pain and heartbreak. Rather than cherish us, they used their words recklessly. They discredited and talked down to us, sowing seeds of worthlessness in our broken hearts. And because our best never met their expectations, we find ourselves still struggling to be "good enough" even today. But your heavenly Father is *nothing* like this.

He looks at you with delight! He's the perfect Father—one who promises to guide you through life with love and compassion. Your relationship with Him will be a source of joy—knowing you're fully known, fully seen, and fully accepted. Friend, you're not alone. Every day, you can experience His goodness working through your life, blessing others, benefitting you, and boasting Him.

....

....

....

....

....

....

....

....

God, thank You for being my perfect Father. That does so
much for my broken heart. In Jesus' name. Amen.

Not for Even a Day

But don't let the passion of your emotions lead you to sin! Don't let anger
control you or be fuel for revenge, not for even a day. Don't give the
slanderous accuser, the Devil, an opportunity to manipulate you!
EPHESIANS 4:26–27 TPT

Our emotions can often get the best of us. When we feel a personal attack or someone we love is hurt by another, our anger can go from zero to sixty in seconds flat. Our usual calm demeanor shifts in a moment as our tempers flare. And it's usually ugly—filled with mean words, finger pointing, vengeful thoughts, and heated exchanges.

The Lord doesn't want anger to control us—not for even a day. He understands human tendencies and wants us to avoid moments that lead to sin. Why? Because that's exactly where the enemy wants us. His plan is to manipulate so our witness for Jesus is compromised. The enemy would love nothing more than to ruin your day. So, when anger is festering, go right to God and ask Him to calm the storm inside.

God, help me to always glorify You with my words
and actions. In Jesus' name. Amen.

Beautiful Gifts

And never let ugly or hateful words come from your mouth,
but instead let your words become beautiful gifts that encourage
others; do this by speaking words of grace to help them.
EPHESIANS 4:29 TPT

Sometimes a kind word is all we need to change the trajectory of our day. Scripture says words have the power to be "beautiful gifts." And when we're struggling, encouragement has a special way of lifting our load and energizing us for the battle ahead.

What friend could use the reassurance right now that everything will be okay? Who needs daily inspiration so they don't give up? Could a coworker use praise for a job well done? Is there someone who needs a cheerleader through a difficult time? Does a friend need a verbal pep rally to get them back in the game of life? Be that kind of woman—the kind who uses words as beautiful gifts. And ask God to give you the eyes to see those who need them.

God, let me be intentional with my words so I use them to bring
encouragement rather than harm. In Jesus' name. Amen.

Don't Give Up

So let's not allow ourselves to get fatigued doing good. At the right time we will harvest a good crop if we don't give up, or quit. Right now, therefore, every time we get the chance, let us work for the benefit of all, starting with the people closest to us in the community of faith.
GALATIANS 6:9–10 MSG

As believers, it's important we have stamina to do God's work every day. There's a beautiful harvest of goodness we'll reap if we don't throw in the towel. But sometimes that's exactly what we want to do. Life gets busy, and our multitasking nature eventually wears us out. And unless we let God strengthen us, we'll give up out of frustration or exhaustion. We need Him to fill us with wisdom, endurance, desire, and every other thing we need to move forward in faith.

Working for the Lord is a privilege, and we should embrace every chance we get to further His kingdom. Every day can be good and productive by remembering that our *yes* to God benefits others in the community of faith.

God, strengthen me to be a blessing to Your kingdom. In Jesus' name. Amen.

Your Source for Success

Make a careful exploration of who you are and the work you have been given, and then sink yourself into that. Don't be impressed with yourself. Don't compare yourself with others. Each of you must take responsibility for doing the creative best you can with your own life.
GALATIANS 6:4–5 MSG

There are few things that promise to ruin your day faster than pride and envy. When your foundation is secured in the truth that all good things come from God, you won't be tempted to pat yourself on the back. Instead, He will get all the credit. You will recognize His hand in your accomplishments. And rather than feel jealous, you'll delight in celebrating others' successes.

Friend, God has given each of us a specific purpose in life. Along with that comes the humility, skill, and grace to walk it out. So, focus on the work God has put before you, and do it with gusto! Ask Him to guide your steps. And recognize the Lord as your source for success.

....

....

....

....

....

....

....

....

....

God, help me do the work You've put before me with humility and gratitude. In Jesus' name. Amen.

Won't Get the Best of You

We are cracked and chipped from our afflictions on all sides, but we
are not crushed by them. We are bewildered at times, but we do not
give in to despair. We are persecuted, but we have not been abandoned.
We have been knocked down, but we are not destroyed.
2 CORINTHIANS 4:8–9 VOICE

Every day is another opportunity for life to punch us in the gut. We are going to face heartache on the regular. And there will be times we're blindsided by betrayal and rejection. Scripture is very clear about it, letting us know that to expect smooth sailing will only lead to disappointment.

But, friend, don't let that ruin your day! When you cling to God, *nothing* will have the power to crush you. Feelings of despair won't linger. You won't be abandoned because God will be with you always. And if you get knocked down, you'll get right back up on your feet, stronger than you were before. Rejoice with a God who won't ever let the world get the best of you.

....
....
....
....
....
....
....
....

God, thank You for reminding me of Your divine protection
and restoration. In Jesus' name. Amen.

Focus on God

So we do not set our sights on the things we can see with our
eyes. All of that is fleeting; it will eventually fade away. Instead,
we focus on the things we cannot see, which live on and on.
2 CORINTHIANS 4:18 VOICE

Today's passage of scripture challenges us to make an intentional decision to focus on God. Because, at the end of the day, He is our only hope. So, keeping our heart connected to Him through the turbulence of life will be what ushers in peace and joy, regardless of what's happening around us.

We so often put our eyes on what's ahead of us when trouble hits. We concentrate on the scary diagnosis and the upended financials. We fix our gaze on all the details surrounding broken relationships. We put a spotlight on the unsettling state of the nation and the world, glued to the television for 24/7 updates that do nothing but cause anxiety. Every day, focus on the one who has the whole world in His hands.

....

....

....

....

....

....

....

....

God, help me keep my heart turned toward You so
fear can't grip it. In Jesus' name. Amen.

Who You Hang Out with Matters

So stop fooling yourselves! Evil companions will corrupt good morals and character. Come back to your right senses and awaken to what is right. Repent from your sinful ways. For some have no knowledge of God's wonderful love.
1 CORINTHIANS 15:33–34 TPT

The truth is simple: you are who you hang out with. And when you spend your days in bad company, the chances are high that your morals and character will be negatively affected. At some point, you will begin to walk a path that leads you away from God. And your focus will be on selfish desires that don't glorify Him. Life is hard enough already without allowing ungodly influences to take hold.

Instead, invest your time in relationships that will encourage your faith. Choose to be around people who point you to God when you're struggling. Build community with those who love the Lord with all their heart, strength, mind, and soul. Make a conscious effort to surround yourself with like-minded people who bring joy and excitement into your life.

....

....

....

....

....

....

God, bring me friends who love You so we can encourage one another! In Jesus' name. Amen.

It's Not Our Place to Judge

"For you'll be judged by the same standard that you've used to judge others.
The measurement you use on them will be used on you. Why would you focus on
the flaw in someone else's life and fail to notice the glaring flaws of your own?"
MATTHEW 7:2–3 TPT

We have no right to judge others. It's not our place to critique or criticize the life of someone else. There's no reason for us to focus on the imperfections of another, especially when we have a bucket full of our own. And, if God's command is for us to love others, sitting in judgment of them is not walking out His will.

Can we be honest and agree this is difficult? We're conditioned to evaluate each other. We're sideline critics and don't even realize it. Ask God to help you be aware of moments when your heart is becoming hard. Let Him guide you away from judgement and into love.

....

....

....

....

....

....

....

....

....

God, help me be a woman who loves others well, not
one full of criticism. Soften my heart to see the good in
those around me. In Jesus' name. Amen.

The Golden Rule

"In everything you do, be careful to treat others in the same way you'd want them to treat you, for that is the essence of all the teachings of the Law and the Prophets."

MATTHEW 7:12 TPT

As the saying goes, "In a world where you can be anything, be kind." Choose to show compassion rather than seek revenge. If there's a need to be met and you're able to meet it, do so with a willing heart. When the Holy Spirit prompts you, be financially generous. Love the unlovable and forgive the unforgivable. Extend grace rather than let bitterness build up. Pray for those around you, especially when you know they're struggling. Because one day, friend, you'll be in a pickle and hoping to be treated in a like manner.

This is the Golden Rule, and it's a worthy pursuit. It's not manipulation. It's not being nice to get something in return. Instead, it's being the hands and feet of Jesus. It's following God's command to love others—and it's an opportunity to make someone's day great.

....

....

....

....

....

....

....

....

God, help me treat others with compassion fueled by Your heart for them. In Jesus' name. Amen.

Living in Such a Way

But exalt Him as Lord in your heart. Always be ready to offer a defense,
humbly and respectfully, when someone asks why you live in hope.
1 PETER 3:15 VOICE

You should live in such a way that others notice that you're different. Every day should be a unique opportunity to point others to God in heaven. What you say in earshot of others matters. The way you act in joy and challenges catches their attention. And, because they know you're a believer, they're looking to see what makes you different. They are watching to see if your faith is real. You are a poster child for Jesus, so be intentional to live in a way that glorifies Him.

Even more, be an authentic representation of what's in your heart. The more time you spend in community with God, the more it will spill into the rest of your life. And that's a beautiful gift to those around you.

....

....

....

....

....

....

....

....

....

....

God, let my life reveal my love for You. Give me the
right words to share in the right moments so others will
follow You too. In Jesus' name. Amen.

Scripture Index

OLD TESTAMENT

NEW TESTAMENT

1 PETER

2 PETER

1 JOHN

Journal Your Way to a Deeper Faith

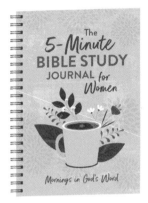

The 5-Minute Bible Study Journal for Women: Mornings in God's Word

In just 5 minutes, you will Read (minute 1–2), Understand (minute 3), Apply (minute 4), and Pray (minute 5) God's Word through meaningful, focused, morning Bible study. *The 5-Minute Bible Study Journal for Women: Mornings in God's Word* includes more than 90 Bible studies that will start your day off right and speak to your heart in a powerful way.

Spiral / 978-1-63609-465-6

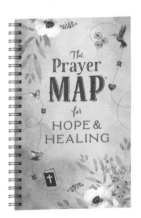

The Prayer Map for Hope and Healing

This engaging prayer journal is a calming and creative way for you to more fully experience the healing power of prayer in your life. Each page features a lovely 2-color design that guides you to write out thoughts, ideas, and lists. . .creating a specific "map" for you to follow as you talk to God.

Spiral / 978-1-63609-424-3